W9-BRX-745

HOME IMPROVEMENT LIBRARY™

The *New*
Everyday
Home Repairs

Simple, Effective Solutions to Your Home's Most Common Problems

CREATIVE
PUBLISHING
international

MINNETONKA, MINNESOTA

Contents

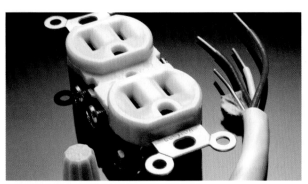

CREATIVE
PUBLISHING
international

Copyright © 2000
Creative Publishing international, Inc.
5900 Green Oak Drive
Minnetonka, Minnesota 55343
1-800-328-3895
www.creativepub.com
All rights reserved

Printed on American Paper by:
R.R. Donnelley & Sons Co.
10 9 8 7 6 5 4 3

President/CEO: Michael Eleftheriou
Vice President/Publisher: Linda Ball
Vice President/Retail Sales & Marketing:
 Kevin Haas

Executive Editor: Bryan Trandem
Creative Director: Tim Himsel
Managing Editor: Michelle Skudlarek
Editorial Director : Jerri Farris

Lead Editor: Philip Schmidt
Copy Editor: Jennifer Caliandro
Senior Art Director: Kevin Walton

Mac Production Artists: Kari Johnston,
 Jon Simpson
Tech Photo Editor: Keith Thompson
Illustrators: Jon Simpson, Rich Stromwall
Director of Production Services: Kim Gerber
Production Manager: Stasia Dorn
Shop Supervisor: Dan Widerski
Studio Services Manager:
 Marcia Chambers
Studio Services Coordinator:
 Carol Osterhus
Photo Team Leader: Chuck Nields
Photographers: Tate Carlson, Andrea Rugg

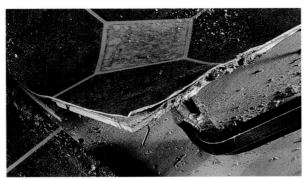

Floors & Stairs 90

Exterior Home Repairs 126

Heating, Ventilation &
Air Conditioning Systems 106

Home Security. 146

Appendix 156

Additional Resources 157

Index 158

Library of Congress
Cataloging-in-Publication Data

The new everyday home repairs : simple, effective
solutions to your home's most common problems.
    p. cm.—(Black & Decker home improvement library)
    Rev. ed. of Everyday home repairs. c1988.
    Includes index.
    ISBN 0-86573-591-3 (soft cover)
    1. Dwellings--Maintenance and repair--Amateurs'
manuals. I. Creative Publishing International.
II. Everyday home repairs. III. Black & Decker
Manufacturing Company (Towson, Md.) IV. Series.

TH4817.3.N49 2000
643'.7--dc21
                            00-023430

THE NEW EVERYDAY HOME REPAIRS
Created by: The Editors of
Creative Publishing international, Inc.
in cooperation with Black & Decker.
BLACK&DECKER. is a trademark of The
Black & Decker Corporation and is
used under license.

Books available in this series:
Decorating With Paint & Wallcovering, Building Decks, Home Plumbing Projects & Repairs, Basic Wiring & Electrical Repairs, Advanced Home Wiring, Carpentry: Remodeling, Landscape Design & Construction, Bathroom Remodeling, Built-in Projects for the Home, Refinishing & Finishing Wood, Exterior Home Repairs & Improvements, Home Masonry Repairs & Projects, Building Porches & Patios, Flooring Projects & Techniques, Advanced Deck Building, Advanced Home Plumbing, Remodeling Kitchens, Stonework & Masonry Projects, Finishing Basements & Attics

Introduction

This is a book of basic home repairs. You'll find it's the source to turn to when the faucet drips, the furnace quits, or a roof leak threatens to turn your ceiling into a floor covering. *The New Everyday Home Repairs* helps you manage emergencies and walks you through easy fix-up projects. Use it when the pipes burst, or when guests are coming and you need to patch a hole in a wall or fix the bathroom door so it latches when you close it.

Whatever the problem, you'll learn how to solve it, quickly and effectively. Each repair in the book gives you clear direction on what materials you'll need, which tools to gather, and how to complete the project, step-by-step, in the most efficient way possible.

To help you find what you need, this book is divided into sections, which together cover your house from top to bottom, inside and out: *Plumbing; Electrical; Windows & Doors; Walls & Ceilings; Floors; Heating, Ventilation & Air Conditioning Systems; and Exterior Home Repairs.* The final section, *Home Security,* gives you advice on assessing your home's security and shows you dozens of ways to deter intruders and protect your home against break-ins. At the end of the book you'll find an appendix with metric conversion tables, a drill bit guide, and lists of resources for further research.

Most everyday repairs can be completed using a few basic tools. Turn to pages 6 and 7 for a look at the hand and power tools that are the most handy to have around the house; you'll also find these and other tools in action throughout the book. Where specialty and rental tools are required for specific repairs, this equipment is displayed in photographs, so you'll know exactly what to purchase, rent, or borrow before you start.

With its color photos and step-by-step instructions, this book is designed as a ready reference to keep open as you complete each repair, but it's best to read through a project before you start. This helps you become familiar with the steps so there won't be any surprises along the way. And be sure to check the *Everything You Need* list of tools and materials found at the beginning of each project. Use this as a checklist for gathering all that's necessary for the job— and to avoid any last-minute trips to the store.

Building a Basic Tool Set

There's a proper tool for every job, and there's one thing to look for in any hand tool: quality. A good tool not only lasts longer than a poor one, it's safer, easier to use, and less likely to damage what you're working on.

While most people buy tools as they need them, keep in mind that some tools, such as open-end wrenches and sockets, are less expensive as a set. And owning a complete set saves you the aggravation of having every tool but the right one.

The tools shown here are the ones you'll use most often. With all the little things that go wrong in a house, none of these tools is likely to sit unused for long.

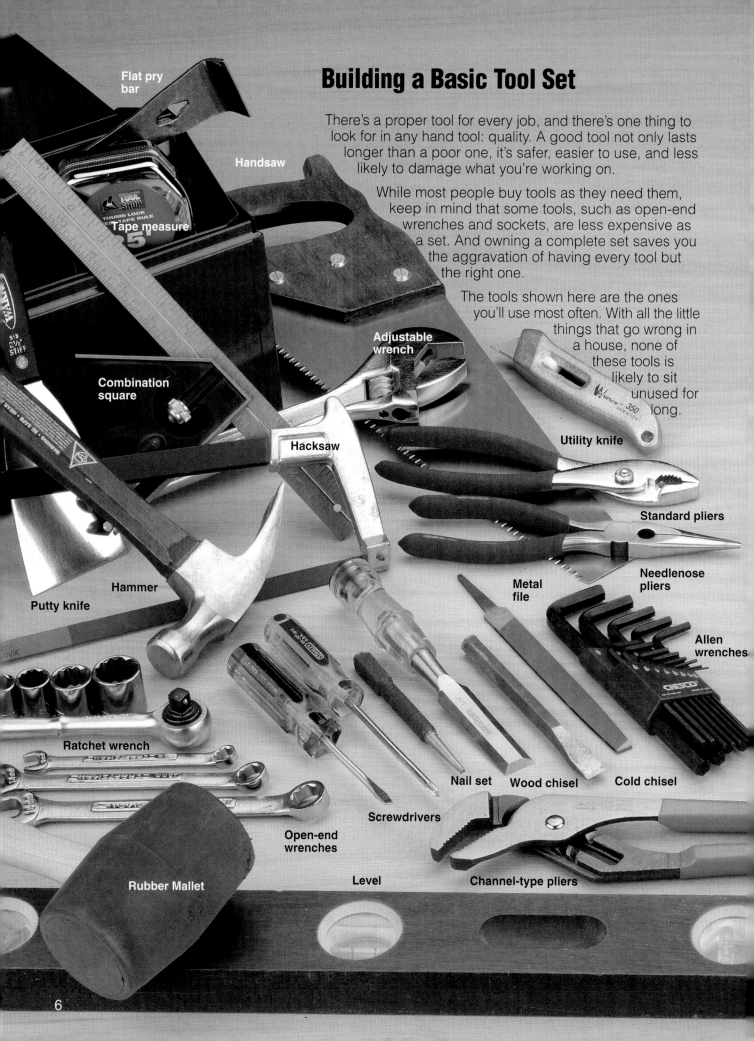

Flat pry bar

Handsaw

Tape measure

Combination square

Adjustable wrench

Hacksaw

Utility knife

Standard pliers

Needlenose pliers

Metal file

Allen wrenches

Hammer

Putty knife

Nail set   Wood chisel   Cold chisel

Ratchet wrench

Screwdrivers

Open-end wrenches

Rubber Mallet

Level   Channel-type pliers

Selecting Power Tools

Despite the higher price as compared with hand tools, power tools are a great value. You'll know this as soon as you put one to use. The time it takes to complete repetitive tasks, like drilling, sawing, and sanding, is reduced dramatically by a good power tool. And for many jobs, power tools are more accurate and easier to use than their manual counterparts—try using a handsaw to make a straight cut through plywood, for example.

For basic home repairs you won't need a fully equipped workshop, but a few of the standard tools will come in handy: A *circular saw* is ideal for any straight wood cuts, square or beveled; *jig saws* cut curves, holes, and slots in most materials; a *palm sander* makes short work of laborious sanding tasks; *cordless screwdrivers* are quick on screws and easy on your wrists; and a *cordless drill*, with a keyless chuck and adjustable speed, is one of the handiest power tools available.

Circular saw

Palm sander

Jig saw

Cordless screwdriver

Cordless drill

7

Plumbing

Making Plumbing Repairs

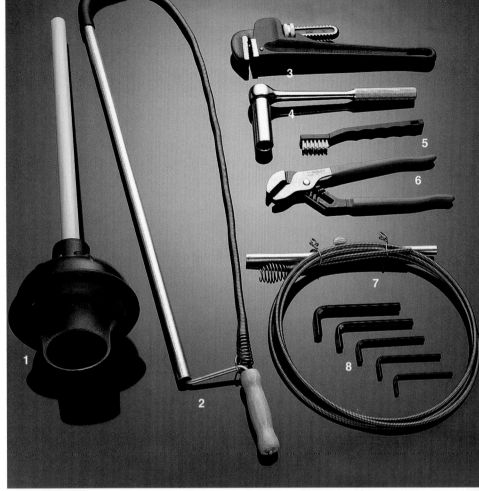

Tools for plumbing repairs include: flanged plunger (1), closet auger (2), pipe wrench (3), ratchet wrench (4), wire brush (5), channel-type pliers (6), drain auger (7), and allen wrenches (8).

The plumbing lines running through your home include two separate systems of pipes. The water *supply* system uses pressure to send clean water to all fixtures via narrow pipes, ½" to 1" in diameter. The drain-waste-vent (DWV) system contains larger pipes, 1¼" or more, and uses gravity, not pressure, to carry waste water from each fixture to the sewer system.

Most plumbing repairs involve leaks or clogs. Leaks are caused by the pressure in the supply system stressing pipes, joints, and fixtures. Clogs form for obvious reasons and because of the lack of pressure in the drain system.

The first rules to remember when making plumbing repairs is to shut off the water at the fixture or the main supply shutoff, and to drain the pipes you will be working on. And always keep a bucket and a rag handy to catch draining water.

How to Shut Off the Water & Drain the Pipes

Individual shutoff valves are found near some fixtures, at the end of the supply tube feeding the fixture. Turn the valve clockwise to stop water flow, then open the faucet or flush the toilet to drain the water. If the fixture has no valve, turn off the water at the main shutoff valve.

The main shutoff valve, located near the water meter, controls the water supply to the entire house. Turn the valve slowly clockwise to close it. Open faucets at the highest and lowest points of the house to drain the pipes.

Fixing Faucets

Most faucets are easy to fix. Replacement parts are inexpensive and readily available at hardware stores and home centers, and you won't need a lot of special tools—just a little patience and attention to detail.

Begin by identifying your faucet type. The most common types are shown here. Don't worry if your faucet doesn't exactly match one of these; it's probably related to one, and you can adapt the repair techniques to work for your faucet. You may have to remove the handle or a cap to identify the faucet type. Look for a setscrew under the handle, or pry off the decorative cap to expose the handle screw.

As you disassemble the faucet, take special note of the orientation of each part. You'll want to reassemble it exactly as it was, lest the faucet give you cold water when you wanted hot and vice versa. And make sure replacement parts match the originals. Parts for popular faucet models are identified by brand name and model number. It's a good idea to bring the worn parts to the store for comparison.

For old faucets, especially compression type, you may have to buy a universal repair kit containing an assortment of neoprene washers, O-rings, packing washers, and stem screws. Just sort through one of these inexpensive kits until you find the parts that fit.

If your faucet isn't leaking but the water flow is weak or irregular, inspect and clean the aerator at the end of the spout (page 17).

Remember to turn off the water at the shutoff valve or main shutoff valve before working on your faucet (page 9).

Everything You Need:

Tools: Channel-type pliers, allen wrench, screwdrivers, utility knife, handle puller (compression type).

Materials: Repair kit or replacement parts, masking tape, heat-proof grease, abrasive pad, packing string (compression type).

Ball-type faucets (page 12) have a hollow ball that controls water temperature and flow. Dripping at the spout is caused by worn valve seats, springs, or a damaged ball. Leaks around the base are caused by worn O-rings. Try tightening the cap before making other repairs.

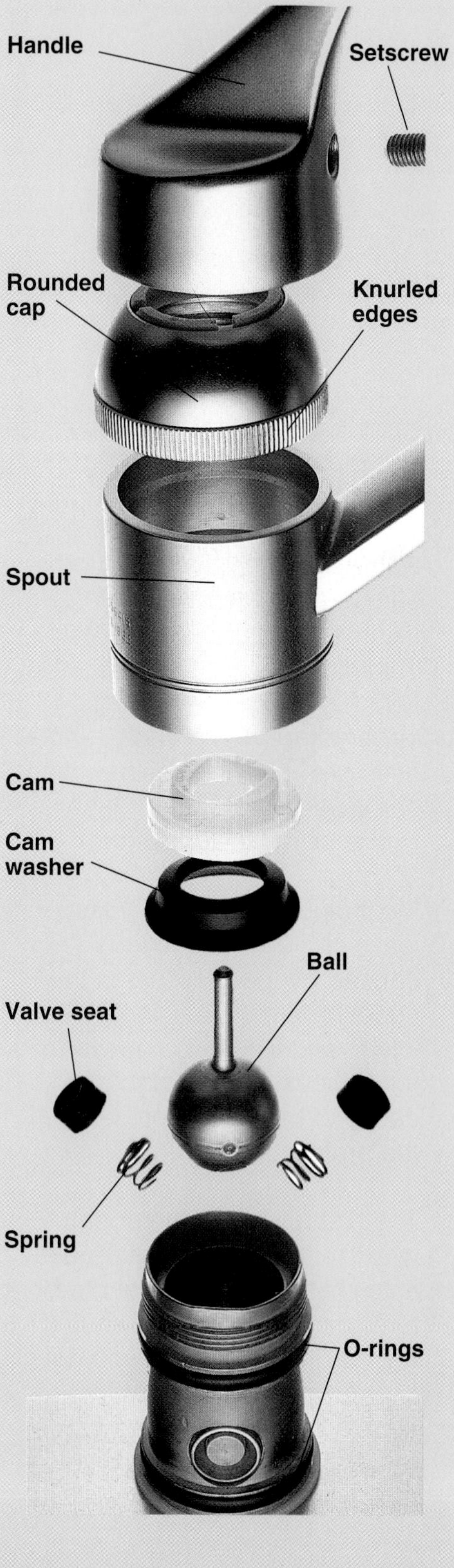

Handle
Setscrew
Rounded cap
Knurled edges
Spout
Cam
Cam washer
Ball
Valve seat
Spring
O-rings

Cartridge faucets (page 13) have a hollow cartridge insert that lifts and rotates to control water flow and temperature. Spout drips are caused by a worn cartridge seal, and leaks around the base indicate worn O-rings. Replacing a cartridge is easy; be sure to align the new one the same as the old.

Disc faucets (page 14) have a sealed cylinder containing two precision ceramic discs. The handle controls water by sliding the discs into alignment. Dripping at the spout occurs when the neoprene seals or cylinder openings are dirty. Replace the cylinder only if the faucet leaks after cleaning.

Compression faucets (pages 15-16) have a stem assembly with a retaining nut, spindle, O-ring, and stem washer and screw. The handle lifts the washer from the valve seat, allowing water into the spout. Spout drips are caused by worn washers, and leaks around the handle by worn O-rings.

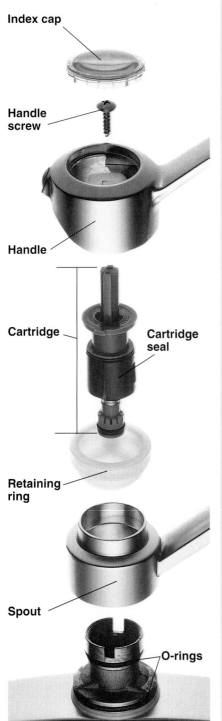

Index cap

Handle screw

Handle

Cartridge

Cartridge seal

Retaining ring

Spout

O-rings

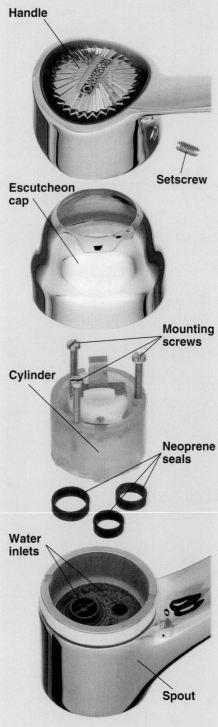

Handle

Setscrew

Escutcheon cap

Mounting screws

Cylinder

Neoprene seals

Water inlets

Spout

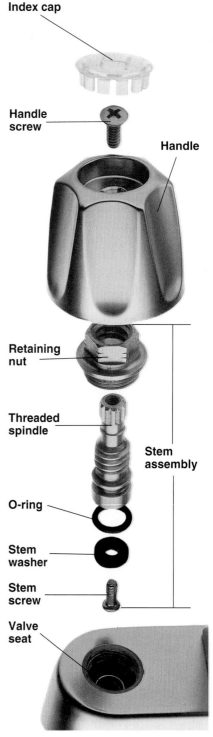

Index cap

Handle screw

Handle

Retaining nut

Threaded spindle

Stem assembly

O-ring

Stem washer

Stem screw

Valve seat

How to Fix a Ball-type Faucet

1 Loosen the handle setscrew with an allen wrench. Remove the handle to expose the rounded faucet cap.

2 Remove the cap with channel-type pliers. To avoid scratching the finish, wrap masking tape around the jaws of the pliers.

3 Lift out the faucet cam, cam washer, and the rotating ball. Check the ball for signs of wear, and replace it only if it is clearly worn or scratched.

4 Reach into the faucet with a screwdriver, and remove the old springs and neoprene valve seats.

5 Remove the spout by twisting it upward, then cut off the old O-rings. Coat the new O-rings with heatproof grease and install them. Reattach the spout, pressing downward until the collar rests on the plastic slip ring. Install new springs and valve seats.

6 Insert the ball, new cam washer, and cam. The lug on the cam should fit into a notch on the faucet body. Reattach the cap and the handle.

How to Fix a Cartridge Faucet

1 Pry off the index cap on top of the faucet, and remove the handle screw underneath the cap.

2 Remove the faucet handle by lifting it up and tilting it backwards.

3 Remove the threaded retaining ring with channel-type pliers. To prevent scratching the ring, wrap masking tape around the jaws of the pliers. Remove any retaining clip holding the cartridge in place.

4 Grip the top of the cartridge with the pliers, and pull straight up to remove the cartridge. Install the replacement cartridge so that the tab on the cartridge faces forward. (If you find the hot and cold controls are reversed, rotate the cartridge 180°.)

5 Remove the spout by pulling up and twisting, then cut off the old O-rings with a utility knife. Coat the new O-rings with heatproof grease and install them.

6 Reattach the spout. Screw the retaining ring onto the faucet, and tighten it with the pliers. Attach the handle, handle screw, and index cap.

How to Fix a Disc Faucet

1 Rotate the faucet spout to the side, and raise the handle. Remove the setscrew, using a screwdriver, and lift off the handle.

2 Remove the escutcheon cap. Remove the cartridge mounting screws, and pull out the cylinder.

3 Remove the neoprene seals from the cylinder openings.

4 Clean the cylinder openings and the neoprene seals with an abrasive pad. Rinse the cylinder with clear water.

5 Return the seals to the cylinder openings, and reassemble the faucet. Move the handle to the ON position, then slowly open the shutoff valves. When the water runs steadily, close the faucet. Ceramic discs can be cracked by bursts of air from the supply system, so be careful.

Install a new cylinder only if the faucet continues to leak after it's been cleaned.

Tips for Fixing a Compression Faucet

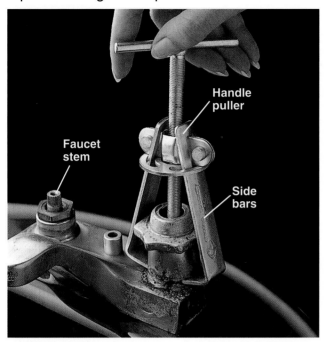

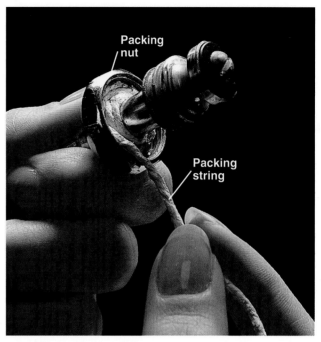

Remove stubborn handles with a handle puller. Remove the faucet index cap and handle screw, then clamp the side bars of the puller under the handle. Thread the puller shaft into the faucet stem, and tighten it until the handle comes free.

Packing string is used instead of an O-ring on some faucets. To fix leaks around the faucet handle, wrap new packing string around the stem, just underneath the packing nut or retaining nut.

Three Common Types of Compression Stems

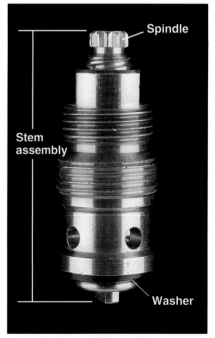

A standard stem has a brass stem screw that holds either a flat or beveled neoprene washer to the end of the spindle. Replace the stem screw if it is worn.

A tophat stem has a snap-on neoprene diaphragm instead of a standard washer. Fix leaks by replacing the diaphragm.

A reverse-pressure stem has a beveled washer at the end of the spindle. To replace the washer, unscrew the spindle from the rest of the assembly. Some stems have a small nut that holds the washer.

15

How to Fix a Compression Faucet

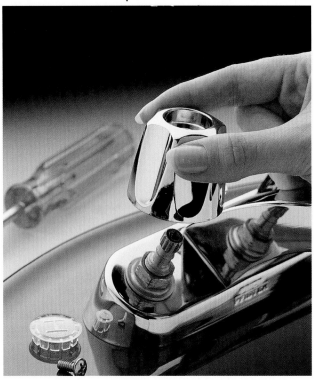 

1 Remove the index cap from the top of the faucet handle, and remove the handle screw. Remove the handle by pulling straight up. If necessary, use a handle puller (page 15).

2 Unscrew the stem assembly from the faucet body, using channel-type pliers.

3 Remove the brass stem screw from the stem assembly. Remove the worn stem washer.

4 Unscrew the threaded spindle from the retaining nut.

5 Cut off the O-ring and replace it with an exact duplicate. Install a new washer and stem screw. Coat all parts with heatproof grease, then reassemble the faucet.

Fixing Sprayers & Aerators

If the water pressure from a faucet or a sprayer head seems low, or if the the flow is partially blocked, unscrew the aerator and clean the parts. The aerator is an attachment with a small metal screen that mixes tiny air bubbles into the water flow.

Sink sprayers are a handy feature on kitchen sinks but are often unused because an old hose has become brittle and difficult to handle. You can fix your old sprayer with an inexpensive replacement hose in a few minutes.

Everything You Need:

Tools: Channel-type pliers, brush, pin, needlenose pliers.

Materials: Vinegar, masking tape, replacement sprayer hose.

Clean aerator parts with a small brush dipped in vinegar to remove mineral deposits. Unplug holes in aerator screens with a straight pin. You can remove most sink aerators with channel-type pliers. Wrap the jaws of the pliers with masking tape to avoid scratching the finish.

How to Replace a Sprayer Hose

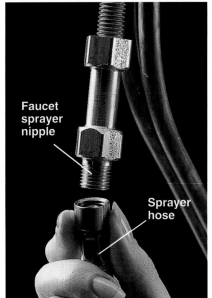

Faucet sprayer nipple

Sprayer hose

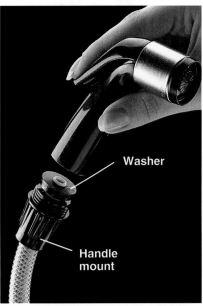

Washer

Handle mount

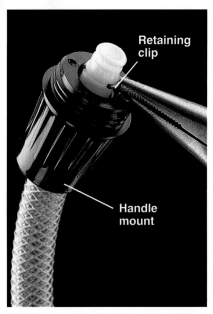

Retaining clip

Handle mount

1 Unscrew the sprayer hose from the faucet sprayer nipple, located under the base of the faucet. Pull the hose through the sink opening.

2 Unscrew the sprayer head from the handle mount, and remove the rubber washer.

3 Remove the retainer clip with needlenose pliers. Attach the handle mount, retainer clip, washer, and sprayer head, then thread the hose through the opening and attach it to the faucet sprayer nipple.

17

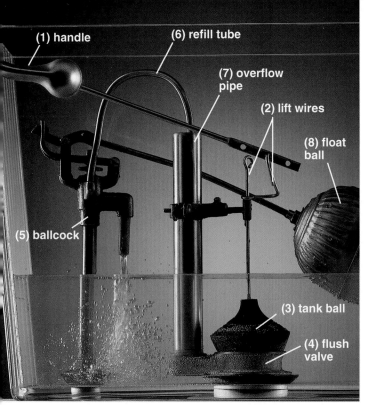

(1) handle **(6) refill tube**
(7) overflow pipe
(2) lift wires
(8) float ball
(5) ballcock
(3) tank ball
(4) flush valve

How a toilet works: When the handle (1) is pushed, the lift wires or chain (2) raise the tank ball (or flapper) (3), allowing water to flow through the flush valve (4) and into the bowl. When the tank is empty, the ball or flapper drops to seal the flush valve. The ballcock (5) refills the tank while the refill tube (6) sends water down the overflow pipe (7) to refill the bowl. The float ball (8) rises with the water and closes the ballcock when the tank reaches capacity.

Repairing Standard Toilets

Common toilet problems include rough handle action, running water, or a sluggish or incomplete flush. Another type of problem—a clogged toilet drain—is covered on page 27. Turn to page 22 for help with pressure-assisted toilets.

Most toilet problems involve the water intake valve, known as the *ballcock*, the handle and lifting linkage, or the *flush valve.* Adjust the handle and linkage to improve flushing action, and make sure the water level is set correctly. If that doesn't add power to the flush, there's probably a partial clog somewhere.

If the toilet runs continuously, remove the tank cover, flush, and watch the system complete a cycle. Make sure the *float device* doesn't touch the tank wall. When the tank is full, lift up on the float device. If this stops the water, you need to adjust the water level so it's just below the top of the *overflow tube.* If the water doesn't stop, repair or replace the ballcock.

If the tank refills intermittently without being flushed, clean and adjust the flush valve, and replace the flapper or tank ball, if necessary.

Everything You Need:

Tools: Adjustable wrench, screwdrivers, stiff brush.

Materials: (as needed) Abrasive pad, universal washer kit, ballcock seals, ballcock, tank ball or flapper.

How to Make Minor Adjustments

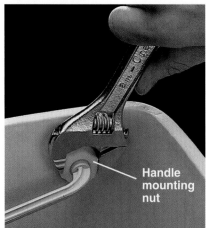

Handle mounting nut

Clean and adjust the handle mounting nut. The nut has reversed threads, so tighten it by turning counterclockwise. Remove lime buildup with a brush dipped in vinegar.

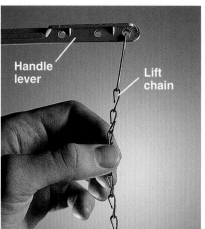

Handle lever   Lift chain

Adjust the lift chain so it hangs straight from the handle lever, with about ½" of slack. Reduce slack by moving the chain to a different hole in the lever or by removing links. Replace a broken chain.

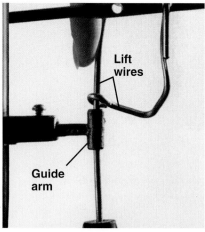

Lift wires

Guide arm

Adjust the lift wires (found on toilets without lift chains), so that the wires are straight and operate smoothly. You may have to adjust the guide arm, but make sure you don't offset the tank ball.

How to Adjust the Water Level

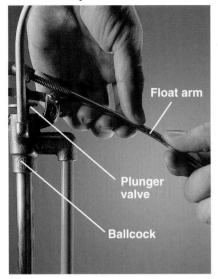

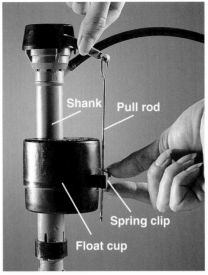

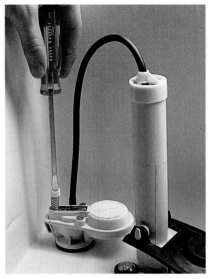

Plunger-valve and diaphragm ballcocks: Lower the water level by bending the float arm downward; bend it up to raise the level. To avoid harmful pressure on the ballcock valve, grasp the float arm in both hands to bend it.

Float cup ballcocks: Pinch the spring clip attached to the pull rod and adjust the position of the cup on the ballcock shank. Move the cup upward to raise the water level; move it downward to lower the water level.

Floatless ballcocks: Use a screwdriver to turn the adjustment screw, ½ turn at a time. To raise the water level, turn clockwise. To lower the water level, turn counterclockwise.

How to Adjust & Clean a Flush Valve

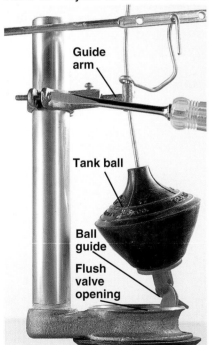

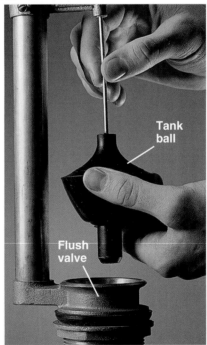

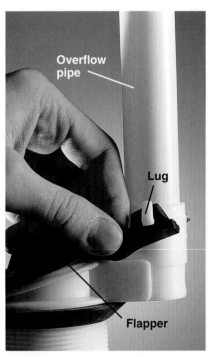

Adjust the tank ball (or flapper) so it is directly over the flush valve. Tank balls have a guide arm for positioning. Some also have a ball guide that helps seat the ball into the flush valve.

Replace the tank ball if it is cracked or worn. Tank balls have a threaded fitting that screws onto the lift wire. Clean the opening of the flush valve, using an emory cloth (for brass) or an abrasive pad (for plastic).

Replace the flapper if it is worn and no longer creates a tight seal. Flappers attach to small lugs on the sides of the overflow pipe.

How to Repair a Plunger-valve Ballcock

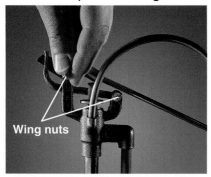

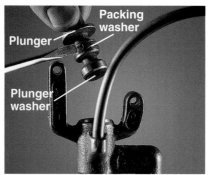

1 Shut off the water (page 9) and flush to empty the tank. Remove the wing nuts on the ballcock. Slip out the float arm.

2 Pull out the plunger. Pry out the packing washer (or O-ring) and plunger washer. Remove the screw holding the washer, if necessary.

3 Install any replacement washers. Clean sediment from inside the ballcock with an abrasive pad. Reassemble the ballcock.

How to Repair a Diaphragm Ballcock

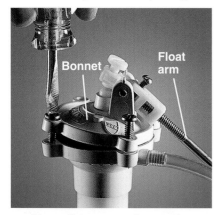

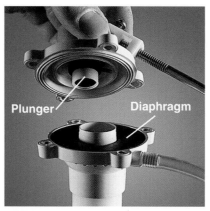

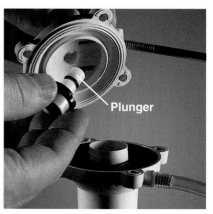

1 Shut off the water (page 9), and flush to empty the tank. Remove the screws from the bonnet.

2 Lift off the float arm with the bonnet attached. Check the diaphragm and the plunger for wear.

3 Replace any stiff or cracked parts. If the assembly is badly worn, replace the entire ballcock (page 21).

How to Repair a Float Cup Ballcock

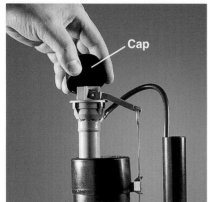

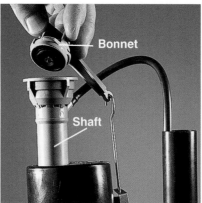

1 Shut off the water (page 9) and flush to empty the tank. Remove the ballcock cap.

2 Remove the bonnet by pushing down on the shaft and turning counterclockwise. Clean sediment from inside the ballcock with an abrasive pad.

3 Replace the seal. If the assembly is badly worn, replace the entire ballcock (page 21).

How to Install a New Ballcock

1 Shut off the water and flush to empty the tank. With a bucket in place to catch water, disconnect the supply tube coupling nut and ballcock mounting nut, using an adjustable wrench. Remove the old ballcock from the tank.

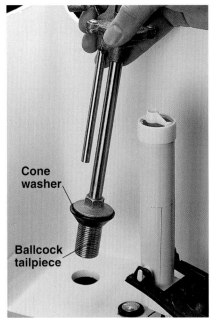

2 Attach the cone washer to the tailpiece of the new ballcock, and insert the tailpiece into the tank opening.

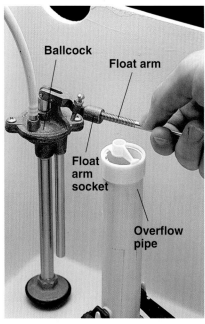

3 Align the float arm socket so the float arm will pass behind the overflow pipe. Screw the float arm onto the ballcock, then screw the float ball onto the float arm.

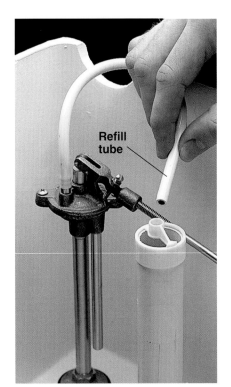

4 Bend or clip the refill tube so the end points straight down into the overflow pipe.

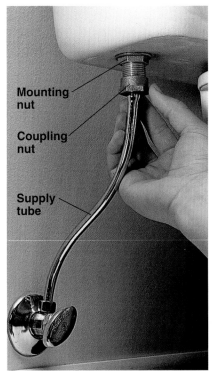

5 Screw the mounting nut and supply tube coupling nut onto the ballcock tailpiece, and tighten them with an adjustable wrench, just until they are snug. Turn on the water and check for leaks.

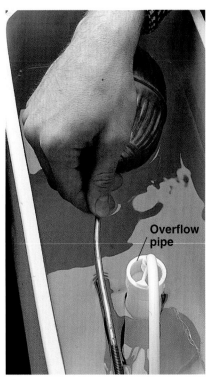

6 Bend the float arm to adjust the water level in the tank so it is about ½" below the top of the overflow pipe (page 19).

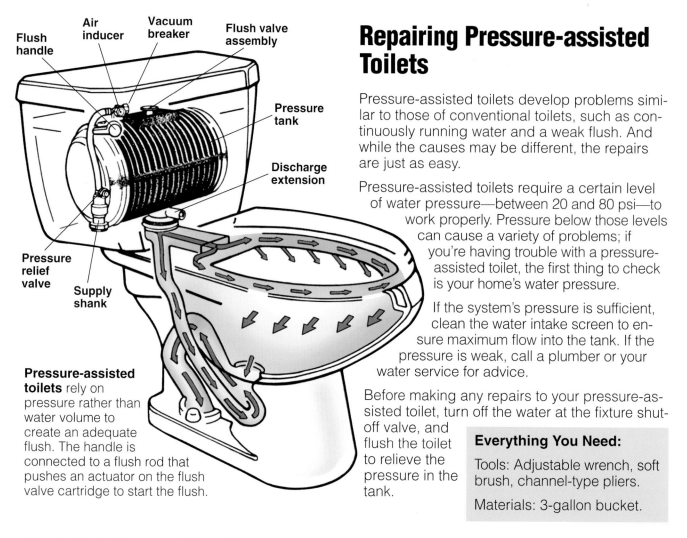

Flush handle
Air inducer
Vacuum breaker
Flush valve assembly
Pressure tank
Discharge extension
Pressure relief valve
Supply shank

Pressure-assisted toilets rely on pressure rather than water volume to create an adequate flush. The handle is connected to a flush rod that pushes an actuator on the flush valve cartridge to start the flush.

Repairing Pressure-assisted Toilets

Pressure-assisted toilets develop problems similar to those of conventional toilets, such as continuously running water and a weak flush. And while the causes may be different, the repairs are just as easy.

Pressure-assisted toilets require a certain level of water pressure—between 20 and 80 psi—to work properly. Pressure below those levels can cause a variety of problems; if you're having trouble with a pressure-assisted toilet, the first thing to check is your home's water pressure.

If the system's pressure is sufficient, clean the water intake screen to ensure maximum flow into the tank. If the pressure is weak, call a plumber or your water service for advice.

Before making any repairs to your pressure-assisted toilet, turn off the water at the fixture shutoff valve, and flush the toilet to relieve the pressure in the tank.

Everything You Need:

Tools: Adjustable wrench, soft brush, channel-type pliers.

Materials: 3-gallon bucket.

How to Test & Improve Water Pressure

1 Turn off the water at the shutoff valve and flush the toilet. Use an adjustable wrench or channel-type pliers to loosen the coupling nut connecting the water supply tube to the supply shank at the bottom of the tank.

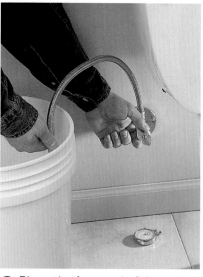

2 Place the free end of the supply tube into a 3-gallon bucket. Mark the time, then open the shutoff valve all the way for 30 seconds. Close the valve and measure the amount of water: there should be more than a gallon.

Supply assembly

Screen

3 Place a bucket under the supply shank. Remove the shank mounting nut, and pull the supply assembly from the tank hole. Inspect the screen inside the shank, and clean it with a soft brush. Reconnect the shank and supply tube.

How to Stop Continuously Running Water

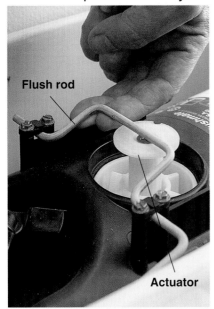

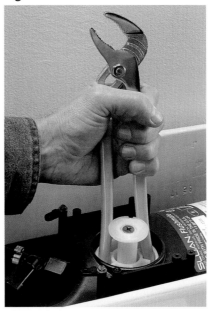

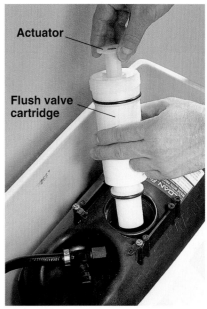

1 Turn off the water at the shutoff valve, and flush the toilet. Lift up on the flush rod: there should be a ⅛" gap between the rod and the top of the actuator. To adjust, loosen the setscrew and rotate the actuator up or down.

2 Unscrew the flush valve cartridge, using the handle ends of channel-type pliers.

3 Inspect the O-rings. If they are worn, replace the cartridge. Reinstall the cartridge, and tighten it. Restore the water supply and let the tank refill. If water runs after refill, depress the actuator: if the flow stops, tighten the cartridge in quarter-turns until the water stops; if flow continues, loosen the cartridge until the water stops.

How to Correct a Weak Flow

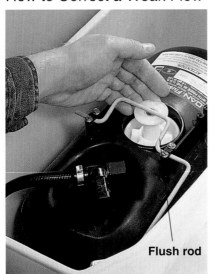

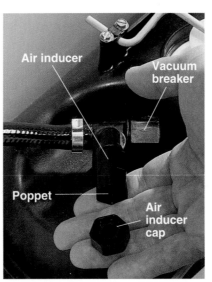

1 With the water supply on, flush the toilet by depressing the actuator. Once the unit begins the flush cycle, carefully raise the actuator. This flushes the system with water to remove debris.

2 Test the air inducer. Remove the inducer cap, and flush the toilet. Look inside the inducer to see that the plastic poppet retracts, and listen for air flow. If there is no flow, unscrew the inducer, and clean the inducer, poppet, spring, and cap.

3 Test for a leaking flush valve cartridge. Turn off the water at the shutoff valve, and flush the toilet. Pour a cup of water into the top of the cartridge, then restore the water supply. If you see a stream of bubbles rising from the cartridge, replace it.

Clearing Clogs & Fixing Drains

Clear a clogged drain with a plunger or a hand auger. A plunger breaks up clogs by forcing air into the drain line. A plunger is effective, simple to use, and easy on the plumbing, so make it your first choice for clearing a clog.

A hand auger has a flexible steel cable that you push and twist through the drain line to break up clogs or snag and remove obstructions. An auger can be messy, but it's fairly easy to use—and a lot cheaper than a plumber. It takes a little practice to get the "feel" of the cable in the drain line, but soon you'll know the difference between an obstruction and a bend in the plumbing.

Use chemical drain cleaners only as a last resort. Available at hardware stores and supermarkets, commercial cleaners will dissolve clogs, but they may also damage pipes and must be handled with caution. Never use chemical cleaners if you have a septic tank.

Clogs and drain repairs go hand-in-hand because it's often necessary to take apart the drain stopper mechanism on a sink or tub in order to reach the clog. If your drain works slowly, try cleaning the stopper assembly. If that doesn't solve the problem, the drain line may be clogged. Sink clogs are often found in the drain trap, which is easy to remove and clean. The trap is also the place to look if you drop a small valuable, such as a ring, down the sink drain.

Everything You Need:

Tools: Plunger, channel-type pliers, wire brush, screwdrivers, pipe wrench, flashlight, hand auger, closet auger, pliers.

Materials: (as needed) Rag, bucket, wire, vinegar, heatproof grease, replacement parts.

How to Clear a Sink Drain with a Plunger

1 Remove the drain stopper. Some pop-up stoppers lift out directly; others turn counterclockwise. On older types, you may have to remove the pivot rod to free the stopper (see below).

2 Stuff a wet rag in the sink overflow opening to prevent air from breaking the suction of the plunger. Place the plunger cup over the drain and run enough water to cover the lip of the cup. Use the handle to move the center of the cup up and down rapidly and forcefully without breaking the seal of the plunger lip.

How to Clean & Adjust a Pop-up Sink Drain Stopper

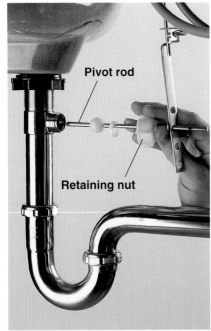

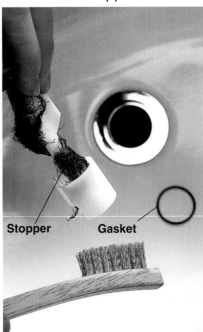

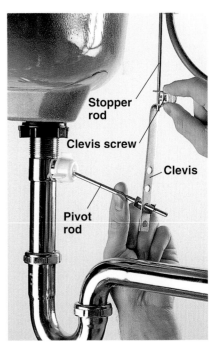

1 Raise the stopper lever to the full upright (closed) position. Unscrew the retaining nut that holds the pivot rod to the sink drain. Pull the pivot rod out of the drain pipe to release the stopper.

2 Remove the stopper. Clean debris from the stopper, using a small wire brush. Inspect the gasket for wear or damage, and replace it, if necessary. Reinstall the stopper.

3 If the sink doesn't drain properly, adjust the clevis. Loosen the clevis screw, and slide the clevis up or down on the stopper rod to adjust the position of the stopper. Tighten the clevis screw.

How to Remove & Clean a Sink Drain Trap

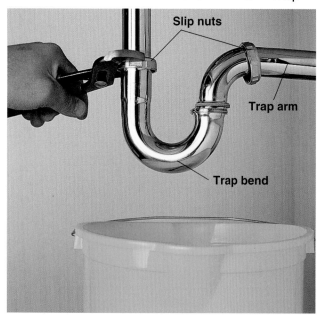

1 Place a bucket under the trap to catch water and waste material. Loosen the slip nuts on the trap bend with channel-type pliers or a pipe wrench. Unscrew the nuts by hand and slide them away from the connections, then carefully pull off the trap bend.

2 Dump out waste material, and clean the trap with a small brush. Inspect the slip nut washers for wear, and replace them, if necessary. Reinstall the trap, and tighten the slip nuts, but do not overtighten.

How to Install a Drain Trap (PVC plastic pipe shown)

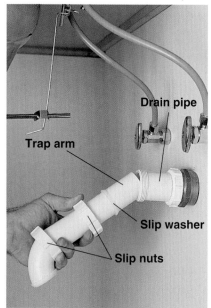

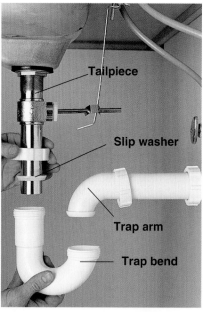

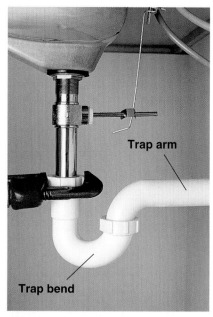

1 Slide the fittings onto the trap arm in this order: slip nut (threads first), another slip nut (threads last), and a slip washer (beveled side last). Push the trap arm about 1½" into the drain pipe.

2 Slide the slip nut onto the sink tailpiece (threads down), then a washer (beveled-side down). Push the long end of the trap bend onto the tailpiece and slide it up until the short end meets the trap arm. Slide the washer and nut down the tailpiece and tighten the nut onto the bend by hand.

3 Move the position of the trap arm to align it with the short end of the trap bend, then tighten all of the nuts with channel-type pliers or a pipe wrench, but do not overtighten. Test the drain by running water. If it leaks, tighten the slip nuts another ¼ turn.

How to Clear a Shower Drain

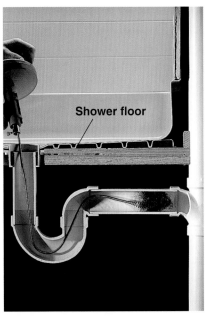

Check for clogs. Remove the strainer cover on the drain, using a screwdriver. With a flashlight, look for hair clogs in the drain opening. Bend a hook-end on a stiff wire and use it to pull hair and other obstructions from the drain.

Use a plunger to clear most shower drain clogs. Place the rubber cup over the drain, and run enough water into the shower to cover the lip of the cup. Work the handle up and down forcefully without breaking the seal of the lip.

Clear stubborn clogs in a shower drain with a hand auger. Use the auger as shown on page 30.

How to Clear a Toilet Drain

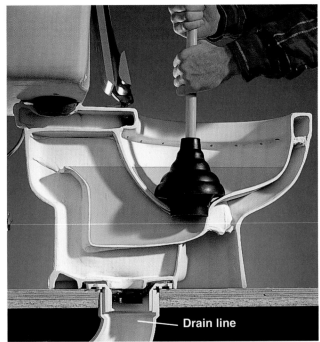

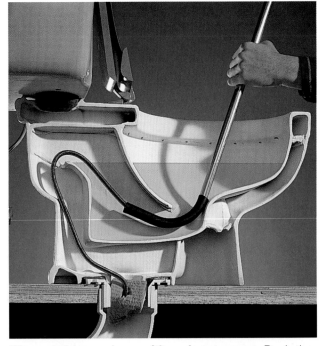

Use a flanged plunger to clear a toilet clog. Place the cup of the plunger over the drain outlet, and plunge up and down rapidly while maintaining a seal around the lip of the cup. Slowly pour a bucket of water (about 2 gallons) into the bowl to clear the drain. Repeat plunging, if necessary, or try a closet auger.

Clear stubborn clogs with a closet auger. Push the auger cable into the trap until the bend seats in the drain opening. Crank the auger handle in a clockwise direction to break up the clog or snag obstructions. Continue cranking as you retrieve the cable to pull the obstruction out of the trap.

How to Identify Tub Drain Types

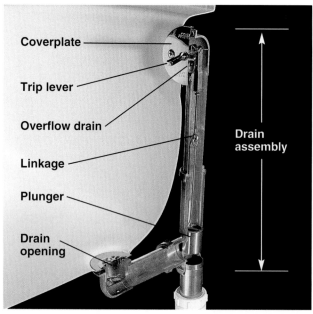

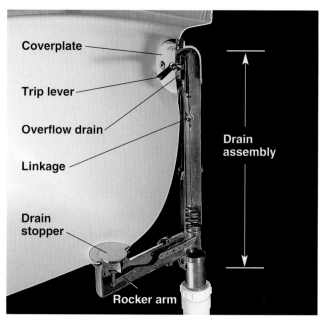

Plunger-type tub drains have a hollow brass plug, called a *plunger*, that slides up and down inside the overflow drain to seal off the water flow. The plunger is controlled by a trip lever and linkage that runs through the overflow drain.

Pop-up tub drains have a rocker arm that pivots to open or close a metal drain stopper. The rocker arm is controlled by a trip lever and linkage that runs through the overflow drain.

How to Clear a Tub Drain with a Hand Auger

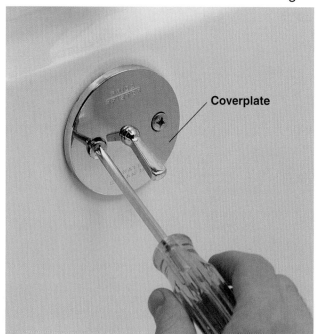

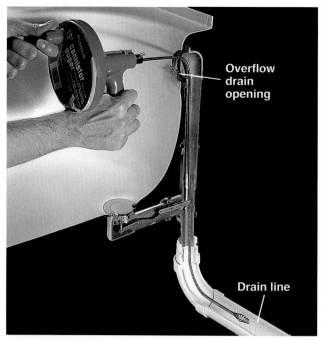

1 Remove the screws on the overflow drain coverplate. Carefully pull the coverplate and drain linkage assembly from the overflow drain (page 29).

2 Feed the auger cable through the overflow opening until you feel resistance. Follow the steps on page 30 to clear the clog. When the drain is clear, replace the linkage, then run hot water to flush the drain.

How to Clean & Adjust a Plunger-type Tub Drain

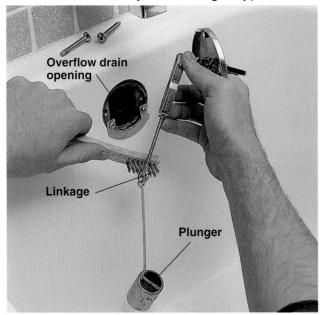

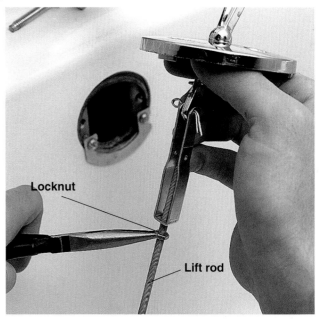

1 Remove the drain overflow coverplate, and carefully pull the coverplate, linkage, and plunger from the overflow drain. Clean the linkage and plunger with a small wire brush dipped in vinegar. Lubricate the assembly with heatproof grease.

2 Increase the drain flow or stop leaks by adjusting the linkage. Unscrew the locknut on the threaded lift rod, using pliers. Screw the rod down about ⅛". Tighten the locknut and reinstall the entire assembly. Readjust the lift rod, if necessary.

How to Clean & Adjust a Pop-up type Tub Drain

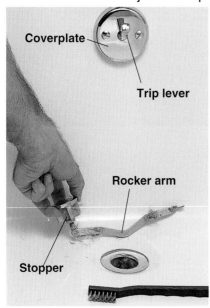

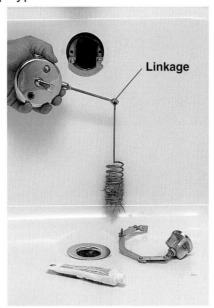

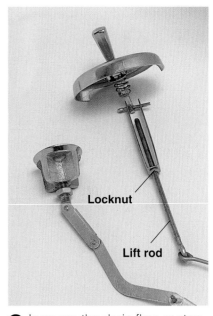

1 Raise the trip lever to the full open position. Carefully pull the stopper and rocker arm assembly from the drain opening. Clean hair and other matter from the rocker arm with a wire brush.

2 Remove the screws from the coverplate, and pull the trip lever and linkage from the overflow drain. Clean the parts with a wire brush dipped in vinegar. Lubricate the linkage with heatproof grease.

3 Increase the drain flow or stop leaks by adjusting the linkage. Loosen the locknut on the threaded lift rod and screw the lift rod up or down about ⅛". Tighten the locknut and reinstall the entire assembly. Readjust the lift rod, if necessary.

How to Clear a Fixture Drain Line with a Hand Auger

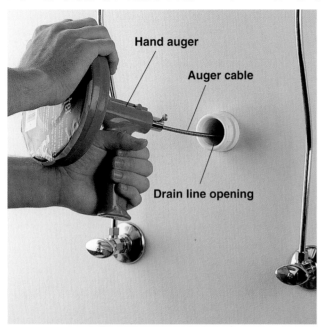

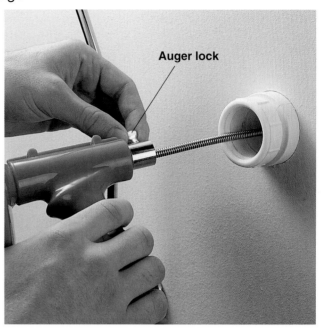

1 Remove the drain trap (page 26). Push the auger cable into the drain line opening until you meet resistance. This resistance usually indicates that the cable end has reached a bend in the drain pipe.

2 Set the auger lock so about 6" of cable extends out of the opening. Grasp the hand grip with one hand and crank the auger handle with the other in a clockwise direction. As you crank, push in on the cable until the end moves past the bend in the drain line.

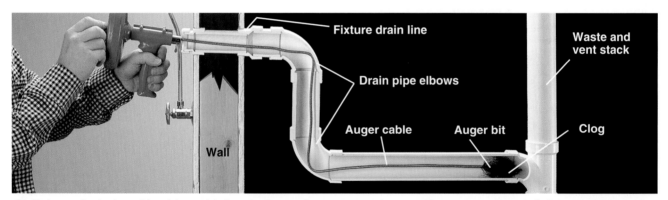

3 Release the lock and feed the cable into the line until you meet resistance. Then, repeat step 2. Solid resistance that prevents the cable from advancing indicates a clog. Try snagging the clog by retracting the cable. Repeat the process, if necessary. Continuous resistance that allows slow advancement is probably a soap clog (step 4).

4 Bore through a soap clog by cranking the auger handle clockwise while applying steady pressure on the hand grip of the auger. Repeat the process two or three times, then retrieve the cable.

Fixing Burst or Frozen Pipes

When a water pipe bursts, immediately turn off the water at the main shutoff valve (page 9). You can temporarily patch burst pipes with a sleeve clamp repair kit, but call a plumber as soon as possible for a permanent repair.

Pipes that freeze but don't burst will block water flow to faucets or appliances. It can save you a lot of trouble—and money—if you thaw the blockage before it breaks the pipe. To find the frozen section, leave blocked faucets or valves turned on, and trace the pipes back from there. Look for places where the line runs close to exterior walls or unheated areas.

Thaw pipes with a heat gun set on LOW, or a hair dryer. Do not use any type of open flame to thaw pipes.

Thaw pipes with a heat gun set on LOW. Keep the nozzle moving so you don't overheat the pipe. Make sure not to overheat flammable materials nearby; use a heat shield if necessary. After the pipe cools, insulate it well beyond the problem area to prevent future freezes. Use sleeve-type foam insulation (shown here) or fiberglass strip insulation and waterproof wrap.

Everything You Need:

Tools: Heat gun or hair dryer, metal file, screwdriver.

Materials: Pipe insulation, sleeve clamp repair kit.

How to Apply a Temporary Patch to a Burst Pipe

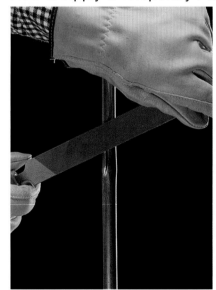

1 Turn off the water at the main shutoff valve (page 9). Thaw the pipe with a heat gun or hair dryer (photo, top left), and allow the pipe to drain. Smooth the rough edges of the rupture with a metal file.

2 Place the rubber sleeve of a repair clamp around the rupture. Make sure any seam is on the opposite side of the pipe from the rupture. Place the two metal repair clamps around the sleeve.

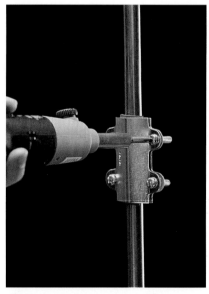

3 Tighten the screws with a screwdriver. Open the water supply and watch for leaks. If the clamp leaks, tighten the screws. **Caution: repairs made with repair clamp kits are temporary. Have the ruptured section replaced as soon as possible.**

Electrical

Making Electrical Repairs

Electricity flows through your home's wiring system much like water flows through plumbing pipes. The electricity travels under pressure through wires to each fixture, is used at the fixture, then flows back along different wires. Like waste water in a plumbing system, returning electricity is not pressurized, and it is said to be at zero *voltage*.

Each electrical *circuit*–a continuous loop of electrical current–contains a "hot" wire, usually colored black, which moves electricity outward from the *main service panel* (see below). A second "neutral" wire, usually white, carries current from the fixture back to the panel. Newer circuits also have a bare copper or insulated green *ground wire*. A single circuit may provide power to one large appliance or to many switches, receptacles, and fixtures.

Everyday electrical repairs usually include replacing or maintaining receptacles, switches, plugs, or light fixtures. These repairs are completely safe as long as you shut off the power to the wires you touch. **Always shut off the power at the main service panel before working with any electrical devices or wires.**

The service panel, or "breaker box," is the metal

Tools for electrical repairs include: cordless screwdriver (1), neon circuit tester (2), insulated screwdrivers (3), continuity tester (4), needlenose pliers (5), fuse puller (6), combination tool (7), and multi-tester (8).

box containing the circuit breakers or fuses for your home's electrical circuits. In newer systems, each circuit is controlled by a *circuit breaker*. Older systems use screw-in plug *fuses*. The main breaker or fuse allows you to turn off all power at once. After switching off the circuit breaker or pulling the fuse to the correct circuit, test any devices or wires you'll be working on with a neon circuit tester (page 34).

If an appliance is not working, make sure the cord is plugged into an active outlet. This may seem obvious but is actually a common "repair."

How to Shut Off Electricity at the Main Service Panel

Circuit breakers control the current in newer wiring systems. Identify the breaker controlling the wires you will touch. Switch the breaker to OFF.

Fuses control the current in older wiring systems. Identify the fuse controlling the wires you plan to work on. Touching the insulated rim only, unscrew the fuse and remove it from the panel.

Cartridge fuses protect circuits for larger appliances. **Use one hand only** to open the panel and handle fuses. If a fuse is housed in a block, grip the handle of the block and pull. Remove fuses from the clips using a fuse puller.

Electrical Safety

Always shut off the power at the main service panel before making any electrical repairs (page 33). After shutting off the power, test the device or wires with a neon circuit tester before touching them. Each repair in this section shows an easy way to test for power before you start.

Electricity is dangerous when it flows outside the established wiring system. By nature, electricity seeks to return to earth along the easiest path. When electrical current finds a path outside the circuit wires—known as a *short circuit*—shock or fire can occur. To protect you and your house from short circuits, your wiring includes a ground system. If circuit wires fail, the ground system provides a safe route for current to follow.

In newer wiring, bare copper or insulated green ground wires run through the system. Circuits may also be grounded through metal electrical boxes and the cables or conduits that connect them, or through ground connections to metal plumbing pipes, which send the current into the earth where it can be absorbed. When making repairs, always reconnect the ground wires.

It's also critical that you use the right materials and properly rated replacement parts for electrical repairs. Always check the ratings for maximum amperage (A) and voltage (V), as well as for wire compatibility (page 35).

Most electrical wire is solid copper, but be aware that your house may have solid aluminum or copper-clad aluminum wire. Circuit cables marked AL or CU-CLAD, and devices marked CU-CLAD ONLY or CO/ALR indicate aluminum wiring. If you suspect your house has aluminum wiring, call an electrician for repairs.

Electrical wire connections not only make the electrical system work, they keep the current running where it should. Loose or exposed wires that cross or contact other materials, such as metal, may cause a dangerous short circuit. Make sure your connections are tight and all wire-to-wire unions are made with properly-sized wire connectors. Use a pigtail (page 36) to connect more than one wire to a single screw terminal.

How to Test for Power Before Making Repairs

1 Test receptacles twice with a neon circuit tester. Shut off the power at the main service panel (page 33). Place one probe of the tester in each receptacle slot. If the tester light glows, the receptacle is still receiving current. Return to the panel and shut off the correct circuit. Test both outlets of a duplex receptacle (shown).

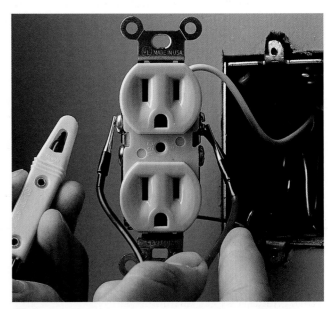

2 Before touching any wires, test the receptacle again. Remove the coverplate and receptacle mounting screws, and carefully pull the receptacle from the box. Touch one probe of the tester to a brass screw terminal and the other to a silver terminal. The tester should not glow. If it does, return to the service panel. If wires are connected to both sets of screw terminals, test both sets.

How to Identify Electrical Materials

NOTE: Position of the screw terminals on switch may vary, depending on manufacturer

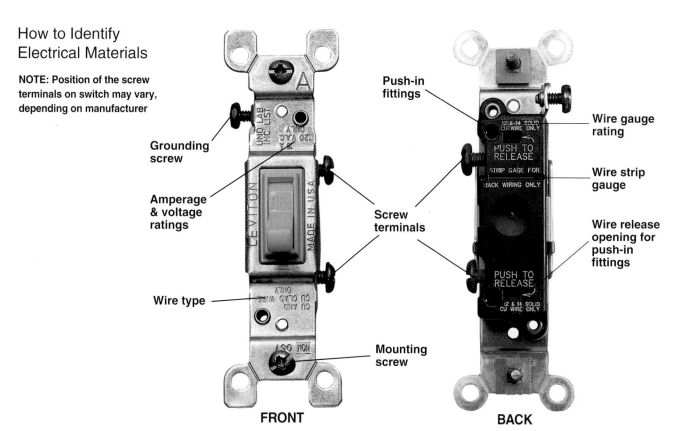

Grounding screw

Amperage & voltage ratings

Wire type

Screw terminals

Mounting screw

Push-in fittings

Wire gauge rating

Wire strip gauge

Wire release opening for push-in fittings

FRONT

BACK

Read the markings on replacement devices to make sure they match the originals. Switches and receptacles marked CU or COPPER are for solid copper wire. Those marked CU-CLAD ONLY are for copper-clad aluminum wire (page 34). Devices marked AL/CU are no longer acceptable for use with any type of wire, according to the National Electrical Code. Standard devices carry amp and voltage ratings of 15A, 125V. For switches and receptacles, voltage ratings of 110, 120, and 125 are considered identical for replacement purposes. You'll also find a specification for wire gauge (size). Standard-voltage devices usually accept #12 or #14 wire. The abbreviation UL or UND. LAB. INC. LIST means the device meets the safety standards of Underwriters Laboratories.

How to Make Electrical Connections

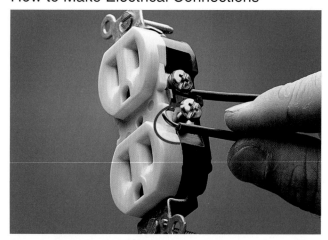

Strip guage

To connect to screw terminals, strip about ¾" from each wire, using a combination tool. Form a C-shaped hook in the wire end with needlenose pliers, then hook the end around the terminal so it forms a clockwise loop. Tighten the screw firmly. The wire insulation should just touch the head of the screw.

To connect to push-in fittings, use the strip gauge on the back of the device to determine how much insulation to remove, then strip the insulation with a combination tool. Insert the wire end all the way into the proper fitting; no bare wire should be exposed. Give a slight tug to make sure the wire is secure. To release a wire, insert a nail or small screwdriver into the release slot and pull the wire free. **Use only properly sized, solid copper wire with push-in fittings.**

How to Use Wire Connectors

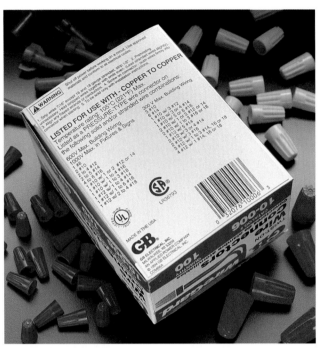

Cut the ends of the wires you are connecting so they are even. Strip about ½" of insulation from each wire, using a combination tool. Hold the wires together and fit the wire connector over the ends; twist it clockwise until it is tight. Metal threads inside the connector grip the wires and keep the connection secure.

Consult the chart on the wire connector package to select the proper size of connector for the gauge and number of wires you are connecting. Wire connectors are colored for easy identification. If there's no chart, use common sense: the connector should be snug and completely cover the bare portions of the wires.

How to Pigtail Wires

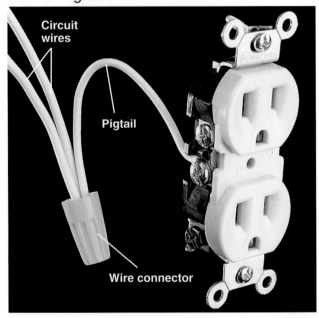

Circuit wires

Pigtail

Wire connector

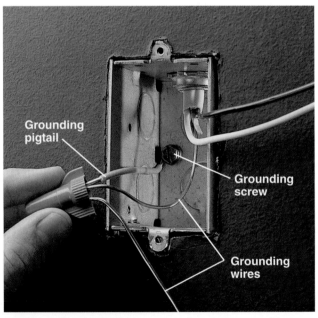

Grounding pigtail

Grounding screw

Grounding wires

Connect two or more wires to a single screw terminal with a short piece of wire, called a *pigtail*, the same gauge and color as the other wires. One end of the pigtail connects to a screw terminal, and the other end connects to the circuit wires. Use a wire connector to join the wires.

A grounding pigtail has green insulation, and is available with a preattached grounding screw. This screw connects to the grounded metal electrical box. The end of the pigtail wire connects to the bare copper grounding wires with a green wire connector.

Replacing Receptacles

Standard receptacles are so inexpensive it's hardly worth repairing a faulty one. If a receptacle is cracked or won't hold a plug firmly, replace it. If a breaker trips or a fuse blows when you plug into a certain receptacle, the circuit could be overloaded, or the plug or appliance could be bad; replace the receptacle if you can rule out those two possibilities.

Because they accept only certain types of plugs and have no grounding hole, you may want to replace old two-slot receptacles. It's also wise to replace very old receptacles that aren't *polarized*, where one slot is longer than the other, because they are likely to be ungrounded and unsafe.

Before you shop for a new receptacle, test the old one for grounding and polarity. A grounding test will tell you what type of receptacle is right–and safe–for a particular outlet. If you find that no means of grounding exists, or if the outlet is in an area where it might get wet, install a GFCI receptacle (page 41). A polarity test reveals whether the hot and neutral wires are connected to the proper terminals. Reversed polarity is a potential hazard that you can correct by rewiring the receptacle.

A standard 125-volt duplex receptacle can be wired in a number of ways. You'll find the most common wiring configurations on page 39. Don't worry if you pull out a receptacle to find a mass of tangled wires; just make sure you label each one before you disconnect it.

Most circuits in your house deliver 120 volts, although some carry 240 volts. These circuits are usually "dedicated" to a high-voltage appliance, such as a clothes dryer or air conditioner. High-voltage receptacles have special slots that won't accept standard plugs. Leave repairs on high-voltage circuits and receptacles to a licensed electrician.

Everything You Need:

Tools: Neon circuit tester, screwdriver.

Materials: Masking tape, pen.

A grounded three-slot receptacle is the modern standard for home electrical systems. Choose a replacement receptacle with the correct amperage (stamped on the receptacle and on the circuit breaker or fuse).

Two-slot polarized receptacles were commonly used before 1960. Polarization is a safety measure that keeps current flowing in the right direction, but it is not a true method of grounding. A two-slot receptacle may be grounded if it is housed in a grounded metal electrical box.

High-voltage receptacles provide 240 volts and 30 to 50 amps to large appliances. Some high-voltage devices are also wired for 125-volt power, for running lower-voltage features, such as lights and timers.

How to Test a Receptacle for Grounding, Polarity & Hot Wires

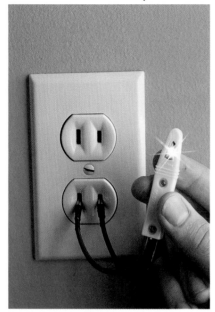

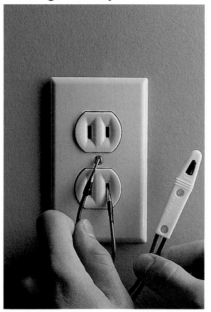

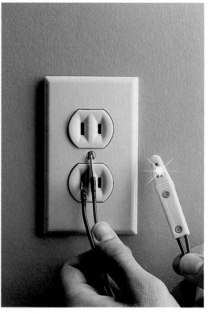

1 To test a two-slot receptacle, leave the power turned on, and place one probe of a neon circuit tester in each slot. If the tester does not glow, there is no power to the receptacle.

2 Place one probe of the tester in the short (hot) slot, and touch the other probe to the coverplate screw. The screw head must be free of paint, dirt, and grease. If the tester glows, the receptacle box is grounded. If it doesn't glow, proceed to step 3.

3 Place one probe of the tester in the long (neutral) slot, and touch the other to the coverplate screw. If the tester glows, the receptacle box is grounded but the hot and neutral wires are reversed. Conduct a test for hot wires (below), then rewire the receptacle (page 40). If the tester does not glow, the box is not grounded.

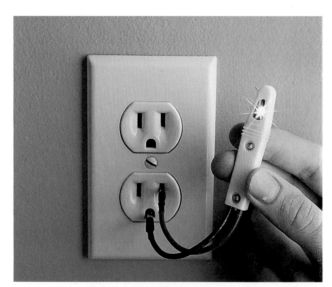

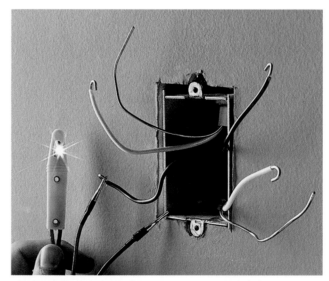

Test a three-slot receptacle for grounding. With the power on, place one probe of the tester in the short (hot) slot, and the other in the U-shaped grounding hole. The tester should glow. If it doesn't, place one probe in the long (neutral) slot and one in the grounding hole. If the tester glows, the hot and neutral wires are reversed. If the tester doesn't glow in either position, the receptacle is not grounded.

Test for hot wires. Occasionally, you may need to determine which wire is hot. With the power turned off, carefully separate all ends of the wires so they do not touch one another or anything else. Restore power to the circuit at the main service panel. Touch one probe of a neon circuit tester to the bare grounding wire or grounded metal box, and touch the other probe to the end of each of the wires. Check all of the wires. If the tester glows, the wire is hot. Turn off the power at the service panel, label the wires, and continue your work.

How to Identify Receptacle Wiring

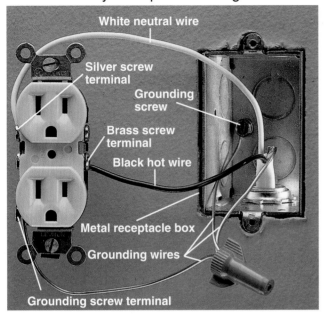

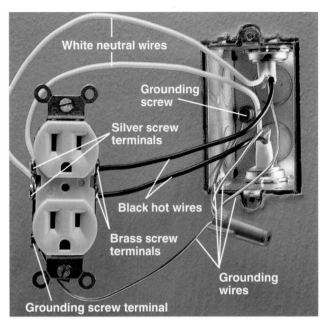

End-of-run wiring is indicated by a single cable entering the box. This means the receptacle is the only, or the last, device in the circuit. The black hot wire is attached to a brass screw terminal, and the white neutral wire is connected to a silver screw terminal. If the box is metal, the grounding wire is pigtailed to the grounding screws of the receptacle and the box. In a plastic box, the grounding wire is attached directly to the grounding screw terminal of the receptacle.

Middle-of-run wiring is indicated by two cables entering the box. Here, the circuit continues to other receptacles, switches, or fixtures. The black hot wires are connected to brass screw terminals, and white neutral wires to silver screw terminals. Or, pigtail wires may link the screw terminals to the circuit wires (page 36). The grounding wires are pigtailed to grounding screws of the receptacle and the box.

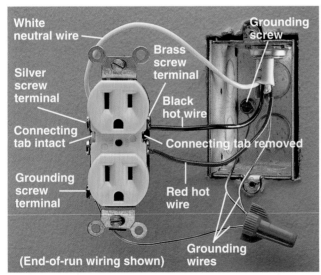

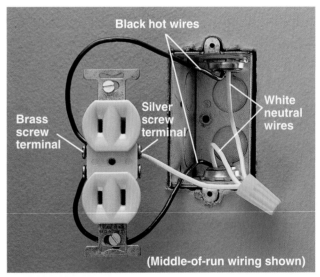

Split-circuit wiring creates two 120-volt circuits from a single 3-wire cable running to a 240-volt circuit breaker. There are two hot wires—one black and one red—connected to the brass screw terminals. The *connecting tab* between the brass terminals is removed. The white neutral wire attaches to the silver terminal, and the connecting tab on the neutral side remains intact. The grounding wire is pigtailed to the grounding screws on the receptacle and the box. This configuration is similar to that of a switch-controlled receptacle.

Two slot receptacles, common in older homes, have no grounding wire attached to the receptacle, but may be grounded through the metal box and cable or conduit. The black hot wires are connected to the brass screw terminals, and the white neutral wires are pigtailed to a silver screw terminal. You can replace a two-slot receptacle with a grounded three-slot type only if the receptacle box is grounded (page 38). If not, you can install a GFCI for protection against a short circuit (page 41).

How to Replace a Standard Receptacle

1 If possible, test the receptacle for grounding and polarity (page 38). Then, turn off the power to the circuit at the main service panel, and test the receptacle for power with a neon circuit tester (page 34). Remove the coverplate and receptacle mounting screws, and pull the receptacle from the box without touching any wires. Test for power again before you begin.

2 Make a masking tape label for each wire, indicating its location on the receptacle screw terminals or push-in fittings. To disconnect the wires, loosen the screw terminals by turning the screw counterclockwise with a screwdriver.

3 Disconnect all of the wires. If more than one wire was connected to a single screw terminal, attach a pigtail, as shown (page 36). Buy a new receptacle that matches the amp and voltage ratings of the circuit.

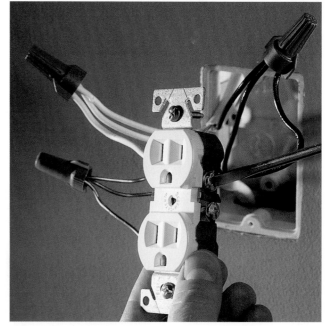

4 Connect each wire to the proper terminal, so the screws are snug, but not overtight. Confirm that all wire connectors are tight, then tuck the wires back into the box, making sure the bare ground wires don't touch the terminal screws. Attach the receptacle, using the mounting screws, and install the coverplate. Restore power to the circuit and test the receptacle with a neon circuit tester.

A GFCI receptacle has a red RESET button and a black TEST button on its face. Test GFCIs monthly by pressing the black button: the red button should click out and shut off the power. Restore power by pressing the red button until it clicks.

Everything You Need:

Tools: Neon circuit tester, screwdriver, combination tool.

Materials: Masking tape, pen, wire connectors, wire.

Installing a GFCI Receptacle

A GFCI (ground-fault circuit-interrupter) receptacle is a safety device. It protects against electrical shock caused by common hazards, such as a faulty appliance or a worn cord, or when plugged-in devices come into contact with water. GFCIs automatically shut off power when they sense small changes in current flow.

Because they can shut themselves off in the event of a short circuit, GFCIs provide security without having to be grounded. This makes them suitable for replacing any duplex receptacle, whether the old one is grounded or not.

A GFCI can be wired to protect itself (single-location) or to protect itself and all devices "down-stream" to the end of the circuit (multiple-location). It can't protect devices between itself and the main service panel. Single-location wiring is preferable, since multiple devices may make a GFCI overly sensitive to false trippings. Consult an electrician for help with multiple-location wiring.

How to Install a GFCI Receptacle for Single-location Protection

1 Shut off power to the receptacle at the main service panel, then follow steps 1-3 on page 40 to remove the old receptacle. Pigtail the white neutral wires together (page 36), and connect the pigtail to the terminal marked WHITE LINE on the GFCI.

2 Pigtail the black hot wires together, and connect the pigtail to the terminal marked HOT <u>LINE</u> on the GFCI. **Caution:** Connecting the black hot wires to the <u>LOAD</u> terminals will prevent proper operation of the GFCI.

3 If the circuit has a grounding wire, connect it to the green grounding screw terminal on the GFCI. Mount the GFCI to the box, and attach the new coverplate. Restore power and test the GFCI according to the manufacturer's instructions.

Repairing Wall Switches

With the exception of dimmers and other specialty switches, most of the wall switches in your house are probably *single-pole* or *three-way* type. Switches are easy to repair or replace, but it's important to know what type you're dealing with.

Single-pole switches are used to control a device, or set of devices, from one location; they have only two screw terminals. This is the most common type of wall switch. Three-way switches control a set of devices from two different locations, are always installed in pairs, and have three screw terminals. (There are also four-way switches, with four terminals, but those are much less common.)

Some switches have a green grounding screw, to which you can attach a pigtail for added protection against shock. Check your local Building Code for rules on grounded switches.

Like receptacles, switches can be wired as *end-of-run* (one cable enters the box), and *middle-of-run* (two cables enter the box) (page 39). With both single-pole and three-way switches, two hot wires connect to the switch screw terminals. Note that in some configurations, the white wire also may be hot. To avoid confusion, be sure to label all of the wires, noting their locations on the old switch, before removing them.

Everything You Need:

Tools: Screwdriver, neon circuit tester, combination tool, continuity tester.

Materials: Sandpaper, masking tape, pen.

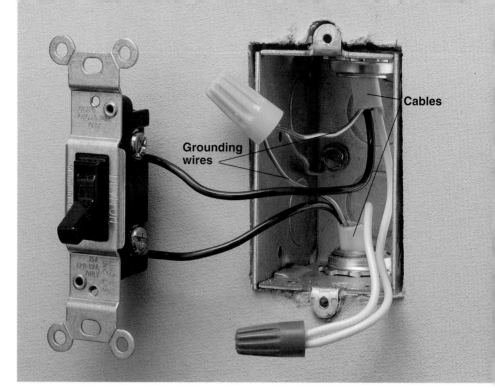

A single-pole switch with middle-of-run wiring, has a black hot wire from each cable attached to a screw terminal. With this configuration, the white wires are neutral and are joined with a wire connector. The grounding wires are pigtailed to the grounded box. See page 43 for end-of-run wiring (sometimes called a *switch loop*).

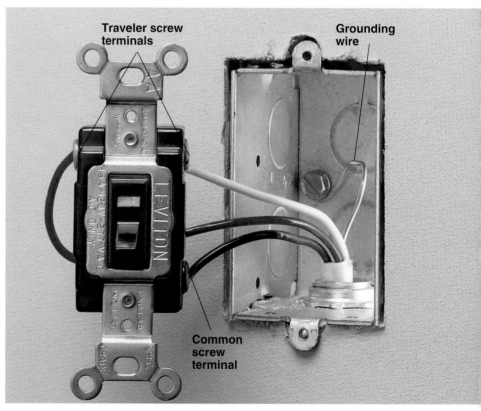

A three-way switch with end-of-run wiring, has a single three-wire cable (plus a ground wire) entering the box. The black hot wire must be connected to the *common* screw terminal, which is darker than the other two. The white neutral and red hot wires are connected to the two *traveler* screw terminals, which are interchangeable. The grounding wire is attached to the grounded metal box. See page 44 for middle-of-run wiring.

How to Repair or Replace a Single-pole Wall Switch (End-of-run Wiring)

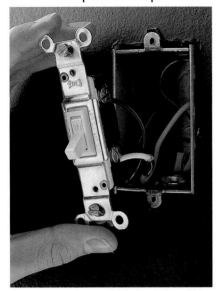

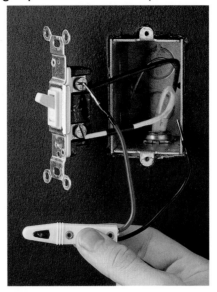

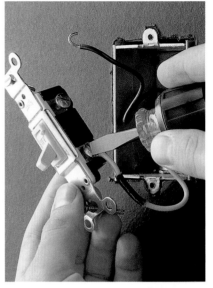

1 Turn off the power to the switch at the main service panel (page 33), then remove the switch coverplate and the mounting screws securing the switch to the electrical box. Without touching any wires, carefully pull the switch from the box.

2 Test for power with a neon circuit tester. Touch one tester probe to the grounded metal box or to the bare copper grounding wire, and touch the other probe to each screw terminal. The tester should not glow. If it does, return to the service panel and shut off the correct circuit.

3 Disconnect the wires from the screw terminals or push-in fittings. **Note:** The mark on the white wire indicates that the wire is hot. This is common with end-of-run switch wiring. If the wire ends are damaged, use a combination tool to clip the end, then strip off about ¾" of insulation. Use sandpaper to clean darkened wire ends.

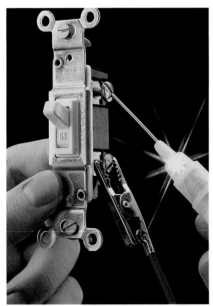

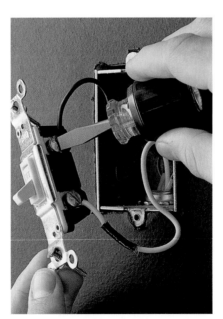

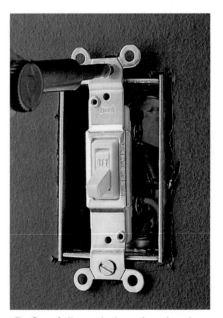

4 Test the switch, using a continuity tester. Attach the tester clip to one screw terminal, and touch the probe to the other terminal. Flip the switch on and off: the tester should glow only in the ON position. If the switch is faulty, buy a replacement with the same volt and amp ratings as the old one.

5 Reconnect the wires to their respective screw terminals. If the wires are too short, lengthen them by adding pigtails (page 36). Tighten the screws firmly, but don't overtighten and strip them.

6 Carefully tuck the wires back into the box, making sure the grounding wire (if there is one) doesn't touch the bare screw terminals. Remount the switch with the mounting screws. Reattach the coverplate, then restore power to the switch.

How to Repair or Replace a Three-way Wall Switch

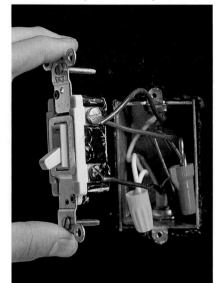

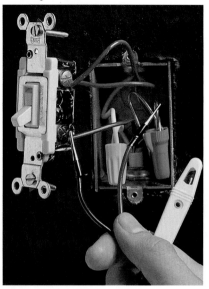

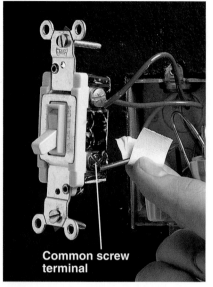

Common screw terminal

1 Shut off power to the switch at the main service panel, then remove the switch coverplate and mounting screws. Without touching any wires, carefully pull the switch from the box.

2 Test for power with a neon circuit tester. Touch one tester probe to the grounded metal box or bare copper grounding wire, and touch the other probe to each screw terminal. The tester should not glow. If it does, return to the service panel and turn off the correct circuit.

3 Locate the common screw terminal: it's darker than the others or is labeled on the switch back. Use masking tape to label the *common* wire attached to the common terminal. Disconnect the wires. If the wire ends are damaged, clip them with a combination tool, then strip off about ¾" of insulation.

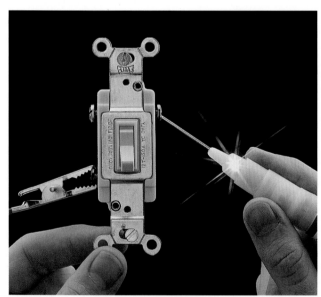

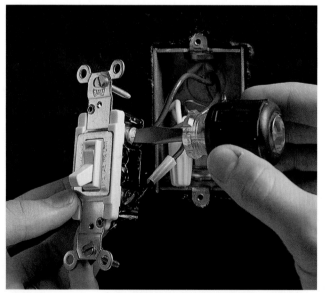

4 Test the switch with a continuity tester. Attach the tester clip to the common screw terminal, and touch the probe to one traveler terminal. Flip the switch lever up and down. The switch tester should glow when the lever is in one position, but not both. Move the probe to the other traveler terminal and flip the lever: the tester should glow when the lever is in the opposite position from the positive test on the first terminal. If the switch is faulty, buy a replacement with the same volt and amp ratings as the old one.

5 Connect the common wire to the common screw terminal. Connect the remaining two wires to the traveler screw terminals; these are interchangeable, but attach only one wire to each terminal. If the wires are too short, lengthen them by adding pigtails (page 36). Tighten the screws firmly, but don't overtighten. Tuck the wires back into the box, making sure the bare grounding wires don't touch the bare screw terminals. Secure the switch with the mounting screws. Reattach the coverplate and restore the power.

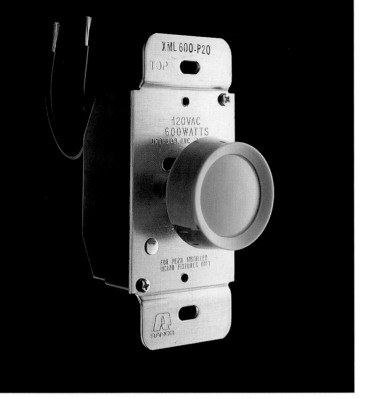

Installing Dimmer Switches

The easiest way to add a dimmer switch is to install it in place of a standard single-pole switch (page 42). After you shut off the circuit and test for power at the switch, check the electrical box to make sure it's big enough for the dimmer switch body and that it isn't crowded with wires. Dimmers have larger bodies than standard switches, and they generate a small amount of heat that needs room to dissipate.

Also be sure to read the manufacturer's instructions for installation specifications and recommended total wattage of the lights controlled by the dimmer.

Dimmer switches have wire *leads* instead of screw terminals, and they connect to circuit wires with wire connectors. Some types also have a grounding lead that connects to the grounded metal box or bare copper grounding wires.

Everything You Need:

Tools: Screwdriver, neon circuit tester, combination tool.

Materials: Standard dimmer switch, wire connectors.

How to Install a Dimmer Switch (End-of-run Wiring)

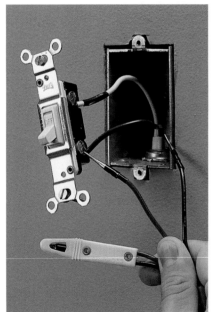

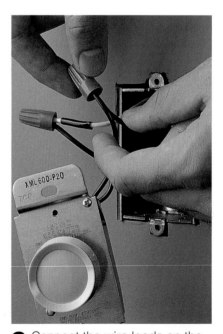

1 Shut off power to the switch at the main service panel. Remove the switch coverplate and mounting screws, and carefully pull the switch from the box without touching any wires. Confirm the power is off with a neon circuit tester (page 43).

2 Disconnect the circuit wires from the switch screw terminals or push-in fittings. Straighten the circuit wires, using a combination tool. Cut the ends, and strip them if necessary, leaving about ½" of bare wire end exposed.

3 Connect the wire leads on the dimmer switch to the circuit wires, using wire connectors. The switch leads are interchangeable and can be attached to either of the two circuit wires. Carefully tuck the wires into the box. Mount the switch and attach the coverplate.

Repairing Incandescent Light Fixtures

Light fixtures can fail because the sockets or built-in switches wear out. Some fixtures have sockets and switches that you can remove for minor repairs, while others have permanently attached parts, and you have to replace the whole fixture when they fail.

One common cause of damage to a light fixture is a light bulb that is rated for higher wattage than the fixture. This can overheat the fixture and burn out the parts.

If a fixture is controlled by a wall switch, check the switch as a possible source of the problem (pages 42-44).

Everything You Need:

Tools: Screwdriver, neon circuit tester, continuity tester.

Materials: Masking tape, pen.

Ground wires

Electrical box

Neutral Wires

Hot wires

Mounting strap

Fixture base

Socket

Shade

A typical incandescent light fixture has one hot and one neutral wire connected to each socket. Newer fixtures have a mounting strap that secures the fixture to the electrical box. This strap should have a preattached grounding screw for attaching the circuit ground wire.

How to Test and Replace a Fixture Socket

1 Turn off power to the fixture at the main service panel. Remove the light bulb, then remove the mounting screws holding the fixture base to the electrical box. Carefully pull the base away from the box without touching any wires.

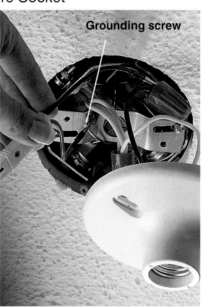

Grounding screw

2 Test for power with a neon circuit tester. Touch one probe to the green grounding screw, and insert the other probe into each wire connector: the tester should not glow. If it does, return to the service panel and turn off the power to the correct circuit.

3 Disconnect the light fixture base by loosening the screw terminals. If the fixture has wire leads instead of screw terminals, remove the fixture base by unscrewing the wire connectors.

How to Test and Replace a Fixture Socket (continued)

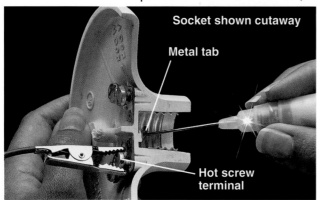

4 Pry up the metal tab in the socket slightly, then test the socket with a continuity tester. Clip the tester to the hot (brass) screw terminal (or black lead), and touch the probe to the metal tab. If the tester doesn't glow, replace the socket or fixture.

5 Attach the tester clip to the neutral (silver) screw terminal (or white lead), and touch the probe to the threaded collar in the socket. The tester should glow. If it doesn't, replace the socket or fixture.

How to Replace a Socket

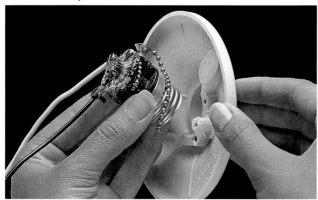

1 Remove the light fixture (steps 1-3, page 46), then remove the socket from the fixture. A socket may be held by a screw, clip, or retaining ring. Disconnect the wires attached to the socket.

2 Buy an identical replacement socket. Connect the white wire to the neutral (silver) screw terminal, and the black wire to the hot (brass) terminal. Attach the socket to the fixture base, and reinstall the fixture.

How to Test and Replace a Built-in Switch

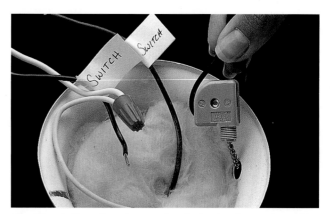

1 Remove the light fixture (steps 1-3, page 46). Unscrew the retaining ring securing the switch to the fixture base. Label the wires connected to the switch leads. Disconnect the wires by unscrewing the wire connectors, and remove the switch.

2 Attach the clip of a continuity tester (see above) to one of the switch leads, and touch the probe to the other lead. Operate the switch control. The tester should glow when the switch is in one position, but not both. Install a duplicate if the switch is faulty.

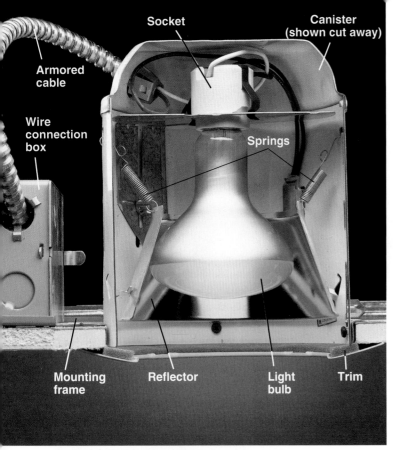

Socket

Canister (shown cut away)

Armored cable

Wire connection box

Springs

Mounting frame

Reflector

Light bulb

Trim

A typical recessed light fixture has a metal mounting frame that holds the fixture in place between framing members. The wire connection box shown here has a push-in type fitting for securing the armored cable.

Testing & Replacing Recessed Light Fixtures

Most problems with recessed lights are caused by heat that builds up inside the metal canister, melting the insulation on the socket wires. Your fixture may have a removable socket that you can take out and replace. If not, replace the entire fixture if the wires are damaged. Buy a replacement fixture that matches the old one, and install it in the metal mounting frame that's already in place.

Unless the fixture is rated *IC* (insulation covered), make sure any building insulation is at least 3" away from the canister, to give the fixture room to dissipate heat.

Everything You Need:

Tools: Screwdriver, neon circuit tester, continuity tester.

How to Remove & Test a Recessed Light Fixture

Spring

Reflector

1 Shut off power to the fixture at the main service panel. Remove the light bulb, trim, and reflector. The reflector is held to the canister with small springs or clips.

2 Loosen the screws or clips holding the canister to the mounting frame. Carefully raise the canister and set it away from the frame opening.

3 Remove the coverplate on the connection box, and test for power with a neon circuit tester. Touch one probe to the grounded box or bare copper grounding wires, and insert the other probe into each wire connector. If the tester glows, return to the panel and shut off the correct circuit.

How to Remove & Test a Recessed Light Fixture (continued)

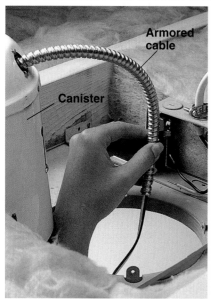

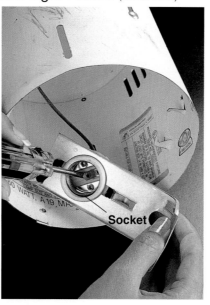

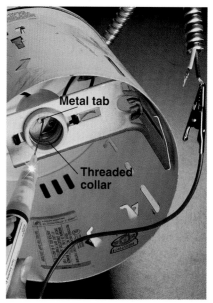

4 Disconnect the white and black circuit wires from the fixture wires by unscrewing the wire connectors. Pull the armored cable from the box, and pull the canister down through the frame opening.

5 Adjust the metal tab at the bottom of the fixture socket by prying it up slightly with a screwdriver. This will improve contact with the light bulb.

6 Test the socket with a continuity tester. Place the clip on the black wire, and touch the probe to the metal socket tab. Move the clip to the white wire, and touch the probe to the threaded collar. The tester should glow for both tests. If it does not, replace the socket or replace the fixture.

How to Replace a Recessed Light Fixture

1 Remove the old fixture (steps 1-4, pages 48-49), and buy a new duplicate fixture. Set the new fixture inside the ceiling cavity, and thread the fixture wires through the opening in the connection box. Push the armored cable into the box to secure it.

2 Connect the white fixture wire to the white circuit wire, and the black fixture wire to the black circuit wire, using wire connectors. Attach the coverplate to the connection box. Make sure any building insulation is at least 3" from the canister and the connection box.

3 Position the canister inside the mounting frame, and attach the mounting screws or clips. Attach the reflector and trim. Install a light bulb with a wattage rating that matches or is lower than the rating indicated on the fixture. Restore power at the main service panel.

Repairing Tracks Lights

Like other light fixtures, track lights are connected to an electrical box in the ceiling. The circuit wires in the box provide power to the entire track, and the current runs along two metal power strips inside the track. Each fixture on the track has a contact arm with metal contacts that draw current from the strips to power the fixture.

Common fixture problems are dirty or corroded contacts or power strips, and bad sockets. Track lights are easy to work on because you can quickly remove individual fixtures to get to the source of the problem.

Everything You Need:

Tools: Screwdriver, continuity tester, combination tool.

Materials: Fine-grit sandpaper, crimp-style wire connectors.

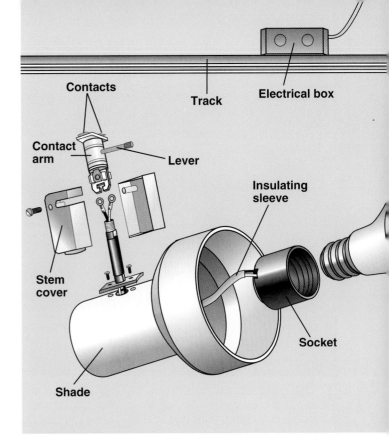

Track lights are powered by an electrical box connected to the middle of, or at the end of, a track. With multiple track sections, special connectors provide the links to power the entire system.

How to Clean Track Light Contacts

1 Turn off the power to the circuit at the main service panel. Shift the lever on the fixture stem to release the fixture from the track. Use fine-grit sandpaper to clean the metal power strips inside the track in the general area where the fixture hangs.

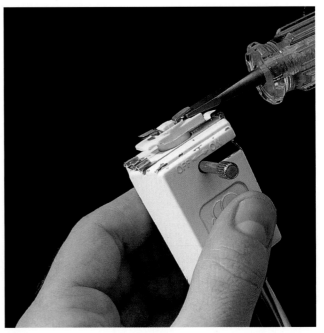

2 Sand the metal contacts on the top of the fixture's contact arm, then use a screwdriver to pry up the tabs slightly. Reattach the fixture to the track, and restore the power. If the fixture doesn't light, test the socket (page 51).

How to Test & Replace a Track Light Socket

1 Turn off the power to the circuit at the main service panel. Remove the problem fixture from the track (page 50). Loosen the screws on the stem cover and remove the cover.

2 Remove the screws securing the socket, and test the socket with a continuity tester. Attach the clip to the brass track contact, and touch the tester probe to the black wire connection on the socket. Repeat the test with the white contact and white wire connection. If the tester fails to light in either test, replace the socket.

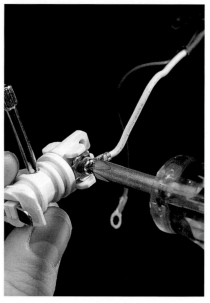

3 To remove the old socket, pull the contact arm from the stem housing, and disconnect the socket wires from the screw terminals. Pull the socket and wires from the shade. If the wires have an insulating sleeve, remove it and set it aside.

4 Buy a replacement socket with the same wattage rating as the old one. Feed the wires of the new socket into the shade and up through the stem. Attach the socket to the shade.

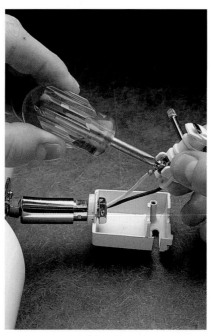

5 Use a combination tool to strip ¼" of insulation from each wire end, and attach a crimp-style wire connector to each wire. Fasten the connectors to the proper screw terminals on the contact arm.

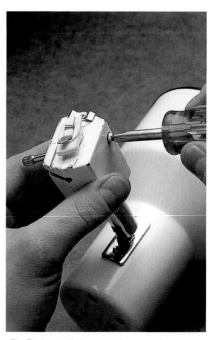

6 Reinstall the socket and contact arm, and reattach the stem cover. Remount the fixture.

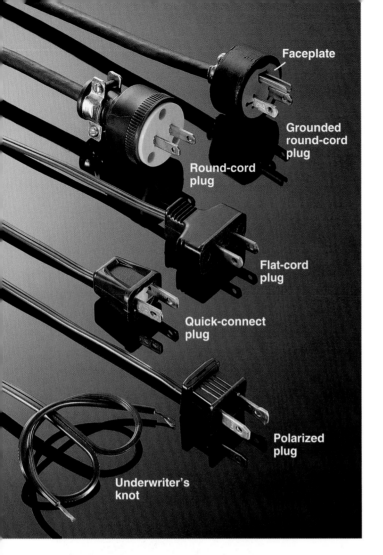

Faceplate

Grounded round-cord plug

Round-cord plug

Flat-cord plug

Quick-connect plug

Polarized plug

Underwriter's knot

Replacing Cord Plugs

Replace an electrical plug whenever you notice bent or loose prongs, a cracked or damaged casing, a missing insulating faceplate, or exposed wires near the plug. All of these pose shock and fire hazards.

Replacement plugs come in different styles; be sure to choose one that has the same features as the original. Flat-cord and quick-connect plugs are suitable for light-duty appliances, such as lamps and radios, and round-cord plugs are used with larger appliances.

Some tools and appliances use polarized plugs, which have one narrow and one wide prong, corresponding to the hot and neutral slots in a polarized receptacle.

If there is room in the plug body, tie the wires together in an *underwriter's knot* to secure the plug to the cord.

Everything You Need:

Tools: Combination tool, needlenose pliers, screwdriver.

Materials: Replacement plug.

How to Install a Quick-connect Plug

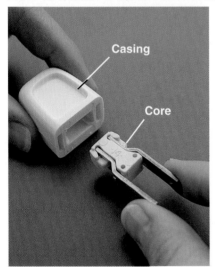

Casing

Core

1 Squeeze the prongs of the new plug together slightly, and pull the plug core from the flat-cord casing. Cut the old plug from the cord with a combination tool, leaving a cleanly cut end.

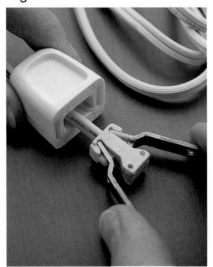

2 Feed the unstripped cord end through the rear of the plug casing. Spread the prongs, then insert the cord into the opening in the rear of the core. Squeeze the prongs together; spikes on the prongs will penetrate the cord. Slide the casing over the core until it snaps into place.

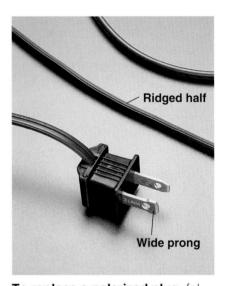

Ridged half

Wide prong

To replace a polarized plug, follow the same basic procedure, and make sure that the ridged half of the cord lines up with the wider (neutral) prong of the plug.

How to Replace a Round-cord Plug

1 Cut off the cord end near the old plug, using a combination tool. Remove the insulating faceplate from the new plug, and feed the cord through the rear of the plug. Strip about 3" of outer insulation from the cord end, then strip ¾" of insulation from each wire.

2 Tie an underwriter's knot (page 52) with the black and white wires. Make sure the knot is located close to the edge of the stripped outer insulation. Pull the cord so that the knot is seated in the plug body.

3 Hook the end of the black wire clockwise around the brass screw, and hook the white wire around the silver screw. On a three-prong plug, attach the third wire to the grounding screw.

4 Tighten the screws securely, making sure the copper wires do not touch each other. Install the insulating faceplate.

How to Replace a Flat-cord Plug

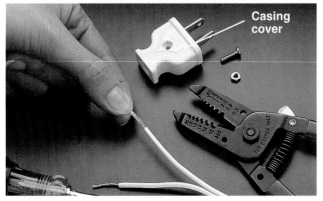

1 Cut the old plug from the cord, using a combination tool. Pull apart the two halves of the cord so that about 2" of wire is separated. Strip ¾" of insulation from each half. Remove the casing cover on the new plug.

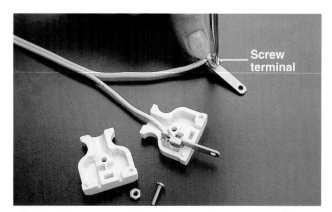

2 Hook the ends of the wires clockwise around the screw terminals, and tighten the screw terminals securely. Reassemble the plug casing. Install the insulating faceplate, if the plug has one.

Repairing Doorbells & Thermostats

Doorbells and whole-house thermostats are similar in that each is powered by a low-voltage *transformer*. A transformer connects to an electrical box or to the main service panel, and it reduces the circuit voltage from 120 volts to anywhere from 15 to 24 volts.

You can identify the transformer for each device by the voltage rating stamped on its face: doorbell transformers rate 20 volts or less and typically are located near the service panel; thermostat transformers rate around 24 volts and are usually found near the furnace or inside the furnace access panel. A thermostat may have an additional transformer controlling an air conditioning unit.

Repairs to either system are easy. You can work with low-voltage wires while the power is on, but shut off the power before replacing a transformer. Start your repairs by conducting a few tests to determine the source of the problem.

A dead doorbell is often the result of a bad switch. If that's not the cause, check the chime unit and the transformer, and test for a break in the low-voltage wiring. Inspect a thermostat for dirt buildup, loose wires, and a failed transformer or thermostat unit. You can replace an old or faulty thermostat with a new programmable type.

As stated, many whole-house thermostats are low-voltage, but there is another type, known as a *line-voltage* thermostat. These are used in zone heating systems, where each room has its own heating unit and thermostat. Line-voltage thermostats typically are powered by a 240-volt circuit, and they have no transformer. Hire an electrician to work on a line-voltage thermostat.

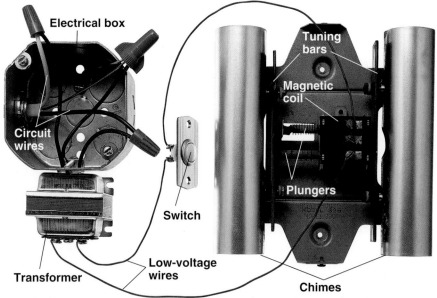

Doorbell systems are powered by a transformer that sends a low-voltage current to one or more push-button switches. When pushed, the switch completes the circuit, activating a magnetic coil in the chime unit and causing a metal plunger to strike the chime.

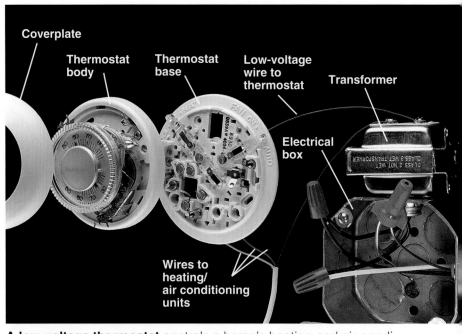

A low-voltage thermostat controls a home's heating and air-conditioning systems. Power leads from a 24-volt transformer to the thermostat on a thin, low-voltage wire. The number of wires leading from the thermostat varies, depending on the type of heating/cooling system.

Everything You Need:

Tools: Screwdriver, continuity tester, multi-tester, pliers, neon circuit tester, soft-bristle paintbrush, combination tool.

Materials: Masking tape, pen, cotton swab, rubbing alcohol, wire.

How to Test a Doorbell Switch

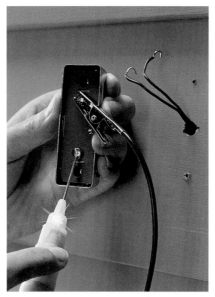

1 Remove the switch mounting screws, and carefully pull the switch away from the wall. If the wire connections are loose, tighten them, then test the switch. If that doesn't work, proceed to step 2.

2 Test the switch with a continuity tester. Attach the clip to one screw terminal, and touch the probe to the other terminal. Press the switch button. If the tester glows, proceed to step 3; if not, replace the switch.

3 Twist the bare ends of the switch wires together temporarily so you can test the other parts of the system. Tape the wires to the wall to keep them from slipping into the wall cavity. Test the transformer (page 56), then inspect the chime unit (below).

How to Test a Doorbell Chime Unit

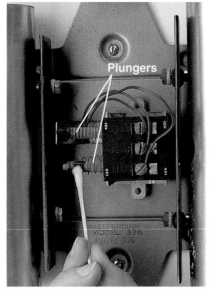

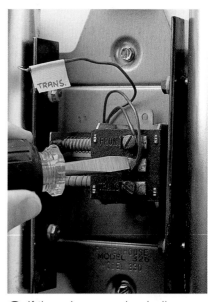

1 If you're sure the switch and transformer are functioning properly, remove the chime coverplate, and clean the plungers with a cotton swab dipped in alcohol. Gummed-up plungers can get stuck and fail to strike the chimes. If the plungers still don't move, proceed to step 2.

2 Test for current with a multitester (page 56). Set the tester to the 50-volt (AC) range. Touch one probe to the terminal marked TRANS and one to the FRONT terminal. The tester should read within 2 volts of the transformer rating. A zero or very low voltage reading indicates a break in the low-voltage wiring.

3 If there is a rear doorbell switch, repeat the test with the TRANS and REAR terminals. If the readings for both tests are within the proper range, the chime unit is faulty. Label the wires and replace the unit.

How to Test a Low-voltage Transformer

 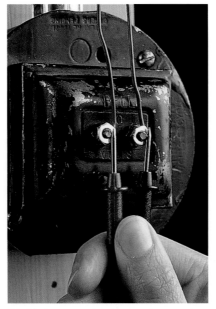 

1 Identify the transformer by the voltage rating on its face (page 54). Shut off the power at the main service panel, then complete steps 1 and 2 below. Reconnect loose wires and replace any tape with wire connectors. Reattach the cover.

2 Make sure the low-voltage wire connections are tight, then turn on the power at the service panel. Set a multi-tester to the 50-volt (AC) range. Touch the probes of the multi-tester to the low-voltage screw terminals on the transformer.

3 If the transformer is operating properly, the multi-tester will detect power that is within 2 volts of the transformer's rating. If the reading is not within this range, replace the transformer.

How to Replace a Low-voltage Transformer

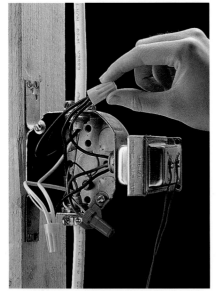  

1 Shut off power to the transformer at the main service panel. Remove the electrical box coverplate. Carefully remove the wire connector on the black circuit wires without touching any bare wire ends.

2 Test for power with a neon circuit tester. Touch one probe to the exposed wire ends, and touch the other probe to the grounded metal box or the bare copper ground wire. Repeat the test with the white circuit wires. If the tester glows for either test, return to the service panel and turn off the correct circuit.

3 Disconnect all wires inside the box and remove the low-voltage wires from the transformer. Unscrew the transformer mounting bracket from inside the box. Buy a replacement transformer with the same volt and amp ratings, and attach it to the box. Connect the circuit wires to the transformer leads, and reattach the coverplate.

How to Test & Replace a Low-voltage Thermostat

1 Turn off the power to the heating/air conditioning system at the main service panel. Remove the thermostat coverplate and clean any dust from the bi-metal coil and other parts, using a soft-bristle paintbrush.

2 Remove the mounting screws securing the thermostat body to the thermostat base, and set the body aside.

3 Inspect the wire connections on the thermostat base, and reattach any loose wires. Restore power to the thermostat, and test the low-voltage transformer supplying the thermostat (page 56).

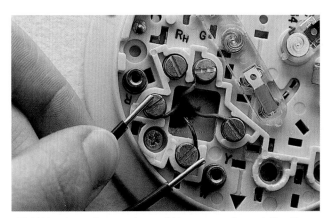

4 If the transformer is working properly, set the thermostat controls to AUTO and HEAT. Strip insulation from the ends of a short wire. Touch the wire to the terminal marked W and the terminal marked R. If the heating system turns on, the thermostat is faulty. Follow steps 5 and 6 to replace the thermostat.

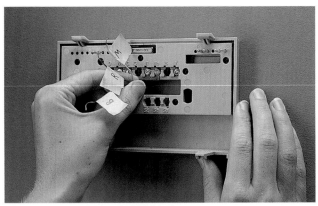

5 Label the wires for their screw terminal locations, then disconnect them and remove the old thermostat. Buy a replacement thermostat that's compatible with your heating/air conditioning system. Thread the wires through the base of the new unit, and mount the base to the wall.

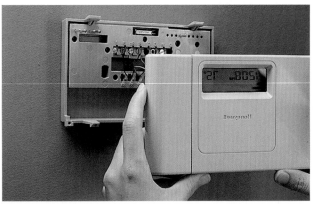

6 Connect the wires to the screw terminals on the thermostat base, using the manufacturer's connection chart as a guide. Mount the thermostat body to the base.

Windows & Doors

Repairing Windows & Doors

There probably isn't a house standing that doesn't have a sticking window or a door that won't close properly. Most windows suffer from a lack of lubrication; the same is true for locksets and other door hardware. The doors themselves, being typically made of wood, swell and warp with humidity, and their hinges loosen due to everyday abuse and the force of gravity. Garage doors, although durable, usually suffer the most from neglect.

If a window is sticking or won't stay open, try one of the simple repairs in this section to improve its operation; the solution may be as simple as cleaning the tracks. Replacing glass and screens also are easy repairs that will improve your windows.

Door problems may require some investigation, but a quick inspection will tell you a lot. Check the gap between the door and the door frame: Is it wider on one side? Can you can feel the door rub against the frame? Is the latchbolt missing the strike plate, or is it just stuck inside the door?

As for garage doors, they thrive on a little routine maintenance. Tightening the bolts and lubricating the moving parts twice a year should prevent most problems. It's also important to check the springs and safety features of your garage door to prevent serious problems.

Cleaners and lubricants for doors and windows include, from left: spray lubricant with Teflon, penetrant/protectant spray, silicone spray, penetrating oil, and all-purpose household oil.

Tools for window and door repairs include: staple gun (1), heat gun (2), drill (3), plane (4), putty knife (5), paint zipper (6), metal file (7), spline roller (8), paintbrush (9), ratchet wrench (10).

Improving Window Operation

Problems with window operation—that is, opening and closing—are specific to the type of window you have. Windows stick if the wood is left unprotected and allowed to swell with moisture, or if someone has painted the window channels. Older windows that won't stay open probably have a broken sash cord or chain.

Newer double hung windows with spring-loaded sash tracks need little maintenance. Clean the vinyl tracks to improve operation, and adjust the springs in (or behind) the tracks, following the manufacturer's directions.

Casement windows cause trouble when the crank mechanisms get dirty or rusty, or when the gears become stripped. If cleaning doesn't fix your casement window, replace the crank mechanism with new parts from the manufacturer or with a generic set you find at the hardware store.

For storm windows, especially the combination type, a little cleaning and lubrication goes a long way. Clean the accumulated dirt from the window track and apply a greaseless lubricant each time you switch the windows and screens.

Everything You Need:

Tools: Screwdrivers, paint zipper or utility knife, hammer, vacuum, small pry bar, scissors, stiff brush.

Materials: Toothbrush, paint solvent, rags, lubricant, wax candle, sash cord, string, all-purpose grease.

How to Adjust Windows

Spring-loaded windows have an adjustment screw found on the track insert. Adjust both sides until the window is balanced and opens and closes smoothly.

Spring-lift windows operate with the help of a spring-loaded lift rod inside a metal tube. Adjust them by unscrewing the top end of the tube from the jamb, then twisting the tube to change the spring tension: clockwise for more lifting power; counterclockwise for less. Maintain a tight grip on the tube at all times to keep it from unwinding.

Tips for Freeing Sticking Windows

Cut the paint film, if the window is painted shut. Insert a paint zipper or utility knife between the window stop and the sash, and slide it down to break the seal.

Place a block of scrap wood against the window sash. Tap lightly with a hammer to free the window.

Clean the tracks on sliding windows and doors with a hand vacuum and a toothbrush. Dirt buildup is common on storm window tracks.

Clean weatherstrips by spraying with a cleaner and wiping away dirt. Use paint solvent to remove paint that may bind windows. Then, apply a small amount of lubricant to prevent sticking.

Lubricate wood window channels with candle wax. Rub a white candle along the channel, then open and close the window a few times. Do not use liquid lubricants on wood windows.

How to Replace Broken Sash Cords

1 Cut any paint seal between the window frame and stops with a utility knife or paint zipper. Pry the stops away from the frame, or remove the molding screws.

2 Bend the stops out from the center to remove them from the frame. Remove any weatherstripping that's in the way.

3 Slide out the lower window sash. Pull knotted or nailed cords from holes in the sides of the sashes (see step 9).

4 Pry out or unscrew the weight pocket cover in the lower end of the window channel. Pull the weight from the pocket, and cut the old sash cord from the weight.

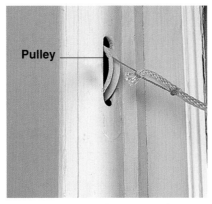

5 Tie one end of a piece of string to a nail and the other end to the new sash cord. Run the nail over the pulley and let it drop into the weight pocket. Retrieve the nail and string through the pocket.

6 Pull on the string to run the new sash cord over the pulley and through the weight pocket. Make sure the new cord runs smoothly over the pulley.

7 Attach the end of the sash cord to the weight, using a tight double knot. Set the weight in the pocket. Pull on the cord until the weight touches the pulley.

8 Rest the bottom sash on the sill. Hold the sash cord against the side of the sash, and cut enough cord to reach 3" past the hole in the side of the sash.

9 Knot the sash cord and wedge the knot into the hole in the sash. Replace the pocket cover. Slide the window and any weatherstripping into the frame, then attach the stops in the original positions.

How to Clean & Lubricate a Casement Window Crank

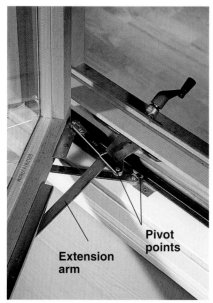

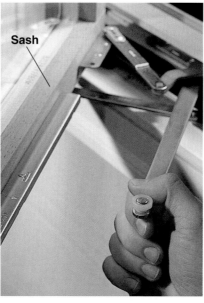

1 If a casement window is hard to crank, clean the accessible parts. Open the window until the roller at the end of the extension arm is aligned with the access slot in the window track.

2 Disengage the extension arm by pulling it down and out of the track. Clean the track with a stiff brush, and wipe the pivoting arms and hinges with a rag.

3 Lubricate the track and hinges with spray lubricant or household oil. Wipe off excess lubricant with a cloth, then reattach the extension arm. If that doesn't solve the problem, repair or replace the crank assembly (below).

How to Repair a Casement Window Crank Assembly

1 Disengage the extension arm from the window track (above), then remove the molding or cap concealing the crank mechanism. Unhinge any pivot arms connected to the window.

2 Remove the screws securing the crank assembly, then remove the assembly and clean it thoroughly. If the gears are badly worn, replace the assembly. Check a home center or call the manufacturer for new parts. Note which way the window opens—to the right or left—when ordering replacement parts.

3 Apply an all purpose grease to the gears, and reinstall the assembly. Connect the pivot arms, and attach the extension arm to the window. Test the window operation before installing the cap and molding.

Replacing Window Glass & Screens

To replace broken glass in a single-pane window, break out the big pieces, wearing gloves and goggles, then wiggle the small pieces out of the glazing. Take the exact dimensions of the window frame opening to the hardware store. Purchase glass that is ⅛" less than the width and length of the opening, to allow for expansion.

Coat the window groove of wood frames with sealant to prevent rot and absorption of oils from the glazing compound. For an easier repair, use the type of glazing compound that comes in a tube.

Replace old screening with new fiberglass screen: it's cheap and easier to install than metal screening. Cut the screen larger than the frame so you'll have something to grip while stretching.

Everything You Need:

Tools: Heat gun, putty knife, caulking gun, sash brush, chisel or screwdriver, utility knife, stapler, hammer, spline roller.

Materials: Gloves, goggles, sandpaper, wood sealer, glazing points and compound, glass, screen, vinyl spline.

How to Replace Window Glass

Putty

1 Remove the window sash, if possible. If not, you can repair it in place. With traditional glazing, soften the old putty with a heat gun, but be careful not to scorch the wood. Scrape away the soft putty with a putty knife. On newer windows, pry out the vinyl glazing strips. If you have metal windows, there should be "spring clip" molding that holds the glass in place; pry this out with a screwdriver.

2 Remove the broken glass and metal glazing points from the frame, then sand the L-shaped groove to clean away old paint and putty. Coat any bare wood with sealer and let it dry.

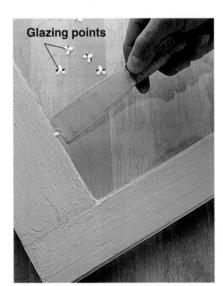

Glazing points

3 Apply a thin layer of glazing compound in the groove. Install the glass and press it lightly to bed it in the compound. Press in new glazing points every 10", using the tip of a putty knife.

4 Apply a bead of glazing compound around the edges of the glass. Smooth the glazing with a wet finger or cloth. When the glazing is dry, paint it to match the window frame. Overlap the paint onto the glass by ¹⁄₁₆" to create a good weather seal.

How to Replace a Screen in a Wood Frame

1 Pry up the screen molding with a small chisel or screwdriver. If the molding is sealed with paint, use a utility knife to cut the film. Cut the new screen 3" wider and longer than the frame.

2 Staple the screen along the top edge of the frame, then stretch it tight and staple it along the bottom edge. Stretch and staple the screen to the sides, one at a time.

3 Nail the screen molding back in place with wire brads or finish nails. Cut away excess screen, using a utility knife.

How to Replace a Screen in an Aluminum Frame

Retaining grooves

1 Pry the vinyl spline from the groove around the edge of the frame with a screwdriver. Retain the old spline if it is still flexible, or replace it with a new spline.

2 Stretch the new screen tight over the frame so that it overlaps the edges of the frame. Keeping the screen taut, use the convex side of a spline roller to press the screen into the retaining grooves.

3 Use the concave side of the spline roller to press the spline into the groove (it helps to have a partner for this). Cut away excess screen, using a utility knife.

Solving Common Door Problems

The most common door problems are caused by loose hinges. When hinges are loose, the door won't hang right, causing it to rub and stick, and throwing off the latch mechanism. The first thing to do is check the hinge screws. If the holes for the hinge screws are worn and won't hold the screws, try the repair on page 68.

If the hinges are tight but the door still rubs against the frame, sand or plane down the door's edge. If a door doesn't close easily, it may be warped—use a long straightedge to check for warpage. You may be able to straighten a slightly warped door, using weights, but severe warpage can't be corrected. Instead of buying a new door, remove the door stop and reinstall it following the curve of the door.

Door latch problems occur for a number of reasons: loose hinges, swollen wood, sticking latchbolts, and paint buildup. If you've addressed those issues and the door still won't stay shut, it's probably because the door frame is out of square. This happens as a house settles with age; you can make minor adjustments by filing the strike plate on the door frame. If there's some room between the frame and the door, you can align the latchbolt and strike plate by shimming the hinges. Or, drive a couple of extra-long screws to adjust the frame slightly (page 69).

Common closet doors, such as sliding and bi-fold types, usually need only some minor adjustments and lubrication to stay in working order.

Door locksets are very reliable, but they do need to be cleaned and lubricated occasionally. One simple way to keep an entry door lockset working smoothly is to spray a light lubricant into the keyhole, then run the key in and out a few times. Don't use graphite in locksets, as it can abrade some metals with repeated use.

Everything You Need:

Tools: Screwdrivers, nail set, hammer, drill, utility knife, metal file, straightedge, pry bar, plane, paintbrush.

Materials: Spray lubricant, wooden golf tees or dowels, wood glue, cardboard shims, 3" wood screws, finish nails, paint or stain, sandpaper, wood sealer.

Latchbolts stick when they are dirty or in need of lubrication. Clean and lubricate locksets (page 67), and make sure the connecting screws aren't too tight—another cause of binding.

A misaligned latchbolt and strike plate will prevent the door from latching. Poor alignment may be caused by loose hinges, or the door frame may be out of square (page 69).

Sticking doors usually leave a mark where they rub against the door frame (page 71). **Warped doors** may resist closing and feel springy when you apply pressure. Check for warpage with a straightedge (page 70).

How to Disassemble and Lubricate a Lockset

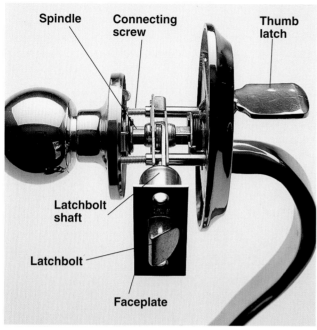

Spindle Connecting screw Thumb latch Latchbolt shaft Latchbolt Faceplate

Connecting screw Spring catch Escutcheon

Modern locksets are sandwiched to the door with two connecting screws; remove these to disassemble the lockset. Spray the moving parts with lubricant, then reinstall the lockset. Tighten the connecting screws an equal amount, but don't overtighten them, which can cause binding.

Some passage locksets have connecting screws hidden behind an escutcheon and often have handles held by a spring catch. To remove the handle, stick a pointed tool into the spring catch hole, then pop off the escutcheon with a screwdriver. Disassemble the lockset and lubricate the moving parts.

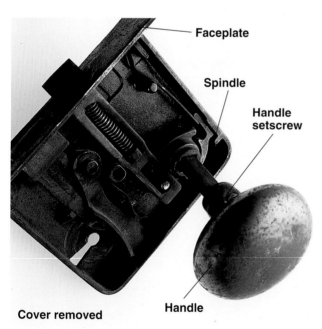

Faceplate Spindle Handle setscrew Cover removed Handle

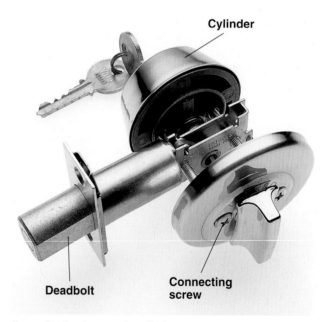

Cylinder Deadbolt Connecting screw

Mortise locksets, common in older homes, are held in place by screws in the faceplate. Remove the faceplate screws, then loosen the setscrew on one of the knobs. Remove the knob, then pull out the other knob and attached spindle, and pry the lockset from the door. Lay the lockset flat and remove the cover without disturbing the internal parts; if you do, just piece them back together. Replace any broken springs and lubricate all of the parts.

Security locks, or deadbolts, usually bind inside the keyed cylinder. Spray lubricant directly into the key-hole and around the deadbolt. Insert the key and turn it several times to spread the lubricant. If that doesn't work, take apart the lock by removing the connecting screws, then lubricate all of the parts.

How to Remove a Door

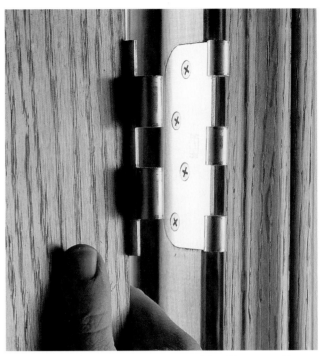

1 Drive the lower hinge pin out, using a screwdriver and hammer. Have a helper hold the door in place, then drive out the upper hinge pin. To help get the screwdriver tip under the pin head, use a nail set or small punch to tap the pin up from underneath.

2 Remove the door and set it aside. Clean and lubricate the hinge pins before reinstalling the door.

How to Tighten Loose Hinges

1 Remove the door from the hinges. Tighten any loose screws. If the wood won't hold the screws tightly, remove the hinges.

2 Coat wooden golf tees or dowels with wood glue, and drive them into the worn screw holes. If necessary, drill out the holes to accept dowels. Let the glue dry, then cut off excess wood.

3 Drill pilot holes in the new wood, and reinstall the hinge.

Tips for Aligning a Latchbolt & Strike Plate

Check the door for a square fit. If the door is far out of square with the frame, remove it (page 68) and shim the top or bottom hinge (right). Or, drive long screws into one of the hinges (below).

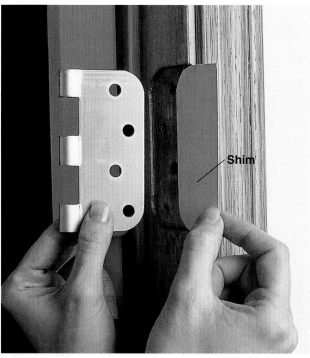

Install a thin cardboard shim behind the bottom hinge to raise the position of the latchbolt. To lower the latchbolt, shim behind the top hinge.

Remove two hinge screws from the top or bottom hinge, and drive a 3" wood screw into each hole. The screws will reach the framing studs in the wall and pull the door up or down. Add long screws to the top hinge to raise the latchbolt or to the bottom hinge to lower it.

Fix minor alignment problems by filing the strike plate until the latchbolt fits.

How to Straighten a Warped Door

1 Check the door for warpage, using a straight-edge. Or, close the door until it hits the stop and look for a gap (see below). The amount of gap between the door and stop reveals the extent of warpage. The stop must be straight for this test, so check it with a straightedge.

2 If the warpage is slight, you can straighten the door using weights. Remove the door (page 68), and rest the ends of the door on sawhorses. Place heavy weights on the bowed center of the door, using cardboard to protect the finish. Leave the weights on the door for several days, and check it periodically with a straightedge.

How to Fix a Severely Warped Door

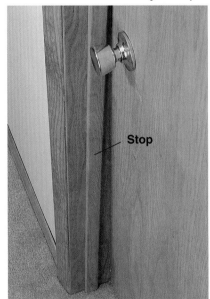

Stop

1 A severe warp cannot be corrected. Instead, you can adjust the door stop to follow the shape of the door. If you touch up the door jamb with paint or stain after you've finished, no one will notice the repair.

2 Remove the door stop, using a small pry bar. If it's painted, cut the paint film first with a utility knife to prevent chipping. Remove nails from the stop by pulling them through the backside of the piece. Pull all nails from the door jamb.

3 Close the door and latch it. Starting at the top, refasten the stop, keeping the inside edge flush against the door. Drive finish nails through the old holes, or drill new pilot holes through the stop. Set the nails with a nail set after you've checked the door operation.

How to Free a Sticking Door

1 Tighten all of the hinge screws. If the door still sticks, use light pencil lines to mark the areas where the door rubs against the door jamb.

2 During dry weather, remove the door (page 68). If you have to remove a lot of material, you can save time by planing the door (step 3). Otherwise, sand the marked areas with medium-grit sandpaper. Make sure the door closes without sticking, then smooth the sanded areas with fine-grit sandpaper.

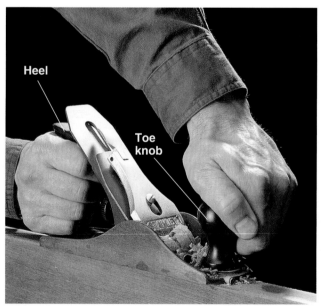

Heel

Toe knob

3 Secure the door on-edge. If the door has veneered surfaces, cut through the veneers with a utility knife to prevent splintering. Operate the plane so the wood grain runs "uphill" ahead of the plane. Grip the toe knob and handle firmly, and plane with long, smooth strokes. To prevent dipping, press down on the toe at the start of the stroke, and bear down on the heel at the end of the stroke. Check the door's fit, then sand the planed area smooth.

4 Apply clear sealer or paint to the sanded or planed area and any other exposed surfaces of the door. This will prevent moisture from entering the wood and is especially important for entry doors.

How to Maintain Sliding Doors

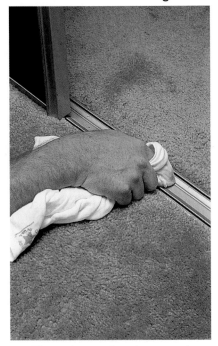

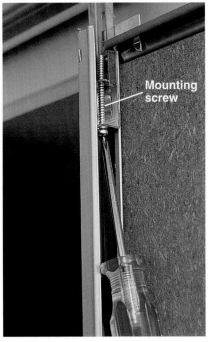

1 Clean the tracks above and below the doors with a toothbrush and a damp cloth or a hand vacuum.

2 Spray a greaseless lubricant on all the rollers, but do not spray the tracks. Replace any bent or worn parts.

3 Check the gap along the bottom edge of the door to make sure it is even. To adjust the gap, rotate the mounting screw to raise or lower the door edge.

How to Maintain Bi-fold Doors

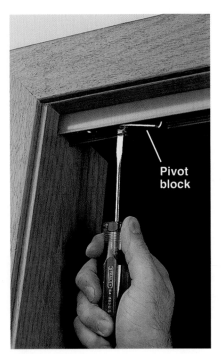

1 Open or remove the doors and wipe the tracks with a clean rag. Spray the tracks and rollers or pins with greaseless lubricant.

2 Check closed doors for alignment within the door frame. If the gap between the closed doors is uneven, adjust the top pivot blocks with a screwdriver or wrench.

Adjustable pivot blocks are also found at the bottom of some door models. Adjust the pivot blocks until the gap between the door and the frame is even.

Replace worn or damaged weatherstripping along the bottom of your garage door. Weatherstripping stops drafts and water, and it protects the door from moisture damage and rot. Nail new stripping in place with galvanized roofing nails. Keep the door panels well sealed with paint or wood sealer to prevent moisture penetration.

Repairing Garage Doors

Garage doors suffer most from moisture, dirt, and neglect. Common symptoms include rusted or rotted panels, loose hinges, squeaky or stuck rollers, and a door that binds or is heavier than usual. Excepting work on the lift springs, you can easily make any garage door repair yourself—and avoid a lot of unnecessary effort.

Start your routine maintenance by cleaning and lubricating the moving parts and tightening all of the hardware. If the door binds or doesn't open smoothly, check the rollers and the track adjustment. Also check the lift springs; a well balanced door should stay open about three feet above the ground; above or below that position, it should open or close by itself. If your door fails this test, call a professional to have the lift springs adjusted or replaced.

Most replacement parts for garage doors, such as rollers, hinges, locks, cables, and hardware, are inexpensive and commonly available at home centers. If you have an automatic garage door opener, always disengage the lifting mechanism by pulling the emergency release cord before making any repairs on the door.

Everything You Need:

Tools: Hammer, ratchet wrench, rubber mallet, level, pliers.

Materials: Weatherstripping, galvanized roofing nails, spray lubricant or oil, replacement hardware.

How to Lubricate a Garage Door

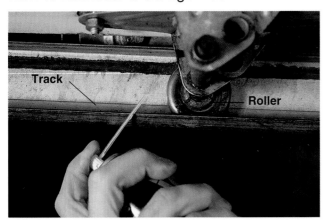

1 Clean the rollers and door tracks with a cloth, then spray them with a greaseless lubricant or apply a small amount of oil. Don't use grease, which attracts dirt. Lubricate door locks, cable pulleys, and hinges.

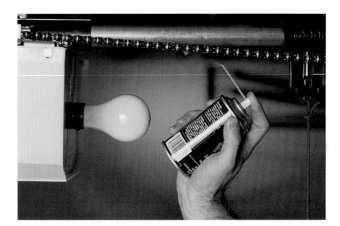

2 Clean and lubricate the chain and track of chain-driven automatic door openers. Openers with other types of drive systems may not require lubrication. Check the manufacturer's instructions for additional maintenance directions.

Tips for Repairing Garage Doors

Tighten all hinge screws or bolts, using a ratchet wrench. Replace any missing or broken hardware and loose or bent hinges.

Adjust the lock so the lock bar meets the lock hole in the door track. Loosen the mounting screws or bolts on the lock to adjust the position of the bar. Center-mounted locks with long lock bars have guides near the door edges. Move the lock bar guides to align the bars with the track holes.

How to Adjust a Garage Door Track

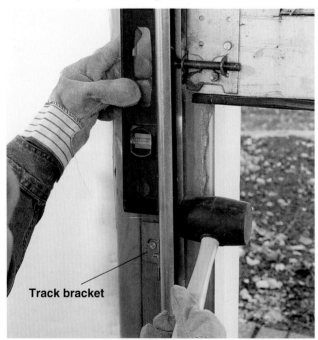

Track bracket

Track bracket

If the door binds in the tracks, loosen the screws securing the lower track brackets to the door framing. Tap the bottom of the track with a rubber mallet to adjust it. Use a level to make sure the track is plumb, then retighten the screws. Adjust both tracks.

If the door rubs against the stop molding, or if there is a large gap, loosen the bolts securing the tracks to the lower track brackets. Adjust the tracks so there's a slight gap between the door and the stop, then retighten the bolts.

How to Replace Garage Door Rollers

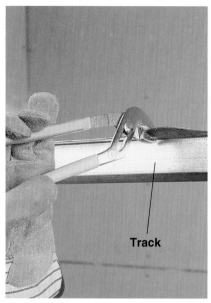

Track

1 Locate the access area on the horizontal portion of each track. Have a helper lift the door until the damaged roller is aligned with the access area. If you can't find an access area, use pliers to bend out a few inches of the top side of the track.

2 Loosen the screws or bolts of the roller hinge, using a ratchet wrench. Tilt the hinge so you can pull the roller out of the track. Replace the hinge if it is bent.

3 Insert the stem of the new roller into the barrel of the hinge, then work the roller into the track. Tighten the hinge mounting screws or bolts.

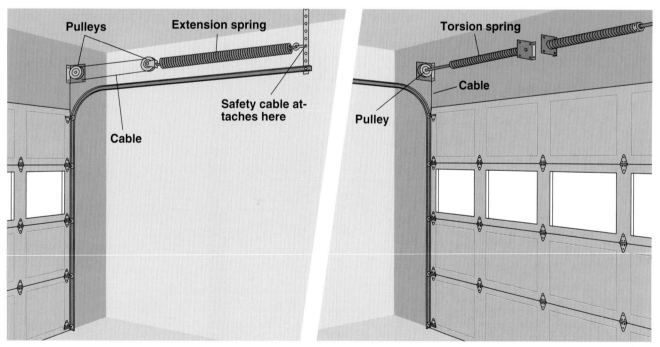

Pulleys   Extension spring

Safety cable attaches here

Cable

Cable

Torsion spring

Cable

Pulley

Garage door lifting mechanisms use powerful steel springs and pulleys and cables to help carry the door's weight. Roll-up doors use one of two spring types. *Extension springs* (left) run parallel to the tracks. The springs are fully "loaded," or under tension, when the door is closed and should be "relaxed" when the door is open. With the door open, check the springs, cables, and pulleys routinely for wear, and call a professional to fix potential problems or to balance the door. Extension springs should have a safety cable that runs through the center of the spring and attaches to the track supports. If you don't have these, get some installed: they prevent the spring from lashing out in the event of a break. *Torsion springs* (right) mount to the wall framing above the door. These are constantly under tremendous tension and should be handled only by a professional.

Walls & Ceilings

Tools & materials for wall & ceiling repairs include: wallboard knives (1), all-purpose wallboard compound (2), latex bonding liquid (3), patching plaster (4) sanding sponge (5), ceramic tile grout (6), fiberglass joint tape (7), wallboard "mud" pan (8), rounded sponge (for tile) (9), wallboard screws (10), rubber grout float (11), wallboard corner bead (12), grout saw and brush (13), wallboard saw (14), and wallcovering seam roller (15).

Repairing Walls & Ceilings

Chances are, most of the wall and ceiling surfaces in your home are either wallboard or plaster. Common problems with these materials are holes, cracks, stains, and water damage. Surface repairs to both materials are easy, but extensive plaster repair—that is, replastering—is not an option for amateurs.

Water damage is a domestic inevitability. Whatever the cause, you'll find symptoms ranging from brown stains and bubbling paint to a collapsed ceiling. (It's not a good idea to poke at a severely damaged ceiling, especially if it's plaster.) Replace water damaged wallboard, if necessary, and have a professional inspect damaged plaster.

Wash moldy surfaces with bleach and trisodium phosphate (TSP) to kill the fungus and prevent it from spreading. If the surface is stained, cover the area with a stain-blocking primer before repainting.

When you've finished your repair and it's time to repaint, cover the area with primer. This seals the dry surface, prevents uneven paint absorption and hides color blemishes or stains that may show through your paint. If your wall or ceiling is textured, use *texture paint* or another texturing product to hide the repair (page 85).

Where walls and ceilings are covered with tile or wallcovering, repairs are important for two reasons: they improve the appearance of the surface, and they protect the underlying plaster or wallboard from moisture penetration.

Tip for Wall & Ceiling Repairs

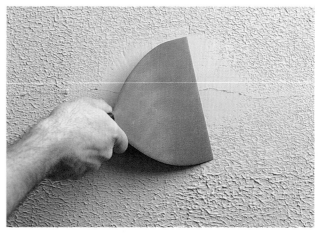

Scrape away texturing with a wallboard knife before making a repair. Patching over a textured surface will result in a less effective and more conspicuous repair. A smooth surface is also easier to retexture.

77

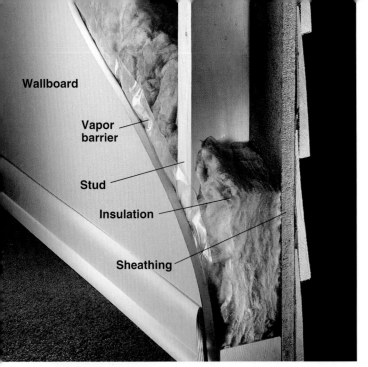

Wallboard

Vapor barrier

Stud

Insulation

Sheathing

Repairing Wallboard

Wallboard, or *drywall*, is easy and inexpensive to repair. For holes, simply cut out the damaged portion and make a patch from a sheet of wallboard. Where fasteners have popped out or where water or gravity has caused a ceiling to sag, you can refasten wallboard panels with screws. There's even an easy way to repair the protective metal edges, called *corner bead*.

Cracks in wallboard occur when a house settles—and usually during the first year after construction—so if your house is new, wait a while before fixing any cracks (page 84).

All wallboard repairs get covered with wallboard compound, which takes a little practice to apply. The most common cause of a noticeable repair is excessive compound. After you spread the compound on the surface, use a wallboard knife to drag it off: think of a rubber spatula scraping batter out of a mixing bowl. Don't worry about covering everything the first time; the compound will stick and fill in where it's needed.

Small repairs take at least two coats of compound, while large repairs may need three or four. Spending an extra hour to fix a hole properly will save you from years of looking at an unsightly patch job. The best thing about the compound is that is sticks to painted surfaces, so you can make spot repairs anywhere, then repaint to blend the patched area into the rest of the wall.

Wallboard panels are fastened to framing members with nails or screws. Panel thicknesses range from ¼" to ⅝", and exterior walls may have a plastic vapor barrier behind the panels. **Beware of pipes and electrical wires when cutting into wallboard. Before cutting, shut off the electrical power to your work area at the main service panel** (page 33).

Everything You Need:

Tools: Drill, hammer, wallboard knives, framing square, wallboard saw, hack saw, file.

Materials: Wallboard screws, wallboard compound, 150-grit sandpaper, wood scraps, fiberglass joint tape, 2 × 4s, washers, metal corner bead, primer, paint.

How to Reset Popped Fasteners

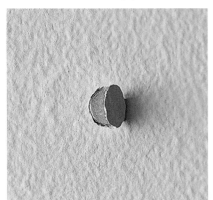

Wallboard fasteners pop when the wood wall framing dries and shrinks. Use screws for repairs: the threaded shanks resist popping.

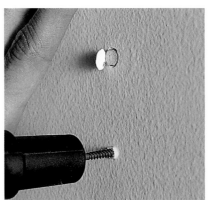

1 Press the wallboard tight against the stud or joist. Drive a screw about two inches from the popped fastener. Recess the screw head slightly, but do not break the face paper on the wallboard.

2 Hammer in the popped fastener, leaving a slight indentation. Fill the dents with two layers of wallboard compound (page 79). Let the compound dry, then repaint.

How to Fill Shallow Dents & Holes

1 Scrape or sand away any peeled paint or wallboard face paper, to ensure a solid base for patching.

2 Fill the hole with lightweight spackle or wallboard compound, using a knife that spans the hole. Allow it to dry. Apply a second coat if necessary to bring the patch flush with the surface.

3 Sand the area smooth with 150-grit sandpaper. Prime and repaint the area to match the surrounding surface.

How to Patch Large Holes

  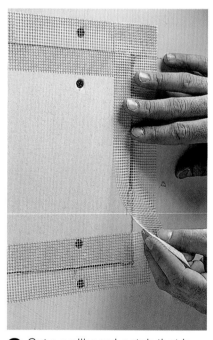

1 Outline the damaged area, using a framing square. (Cutting four right angles makes it easier to measure and cut the patch.) Use a wallboard saw to cut along the outline.

2 Cut backer strips from flat pieces of wood (plywood or board lumber works best). Install the backer strips, using 1¼" wallboard screws.

3 Cut a wallboard patch that is the same thickness as the existing wallboard. Make the patch ⅛" smaller than the dimensions of the cutout. Secure the patch to the backer strips with screws. Apply fiberglass joint tape over the seams.

How to Patch Large Holes (continued)

4 Cover the taped seams with all-purpose wallboard compound, using a 6" wallboard knife. Make a second pass with the knife to press the compound into the seams, and remove excess, leaving a smooth, thin layer. Let the compound dry.

5 Sand or scrape the area lightly to remove any protrusions, then wipe away any dust. Apply a second layer of compound to cover the entire patch area, using a 12" wallboard knife. Make additional passes with the knife, leaving a smooth, thin layer of compound. Let the compound dry. Repeat, if necessary.

Tips for Refastening a Sagging Ceiling

Build a 2 × 4 T-brace to force sagging panels against the ceiling framing. Make the vertical leg of the brace about ½" longer than the distance from the floor to the ceiling. Wedge the brace in place along wallboard seams and close to rows of fasteners. Refasten the panel section with wallboard screws before removing the brace.

Remove water-damaged joint tape from wallboard seams. For badly damaged seams, use broad, thin washers and long screws for refastening. Recess the washers slightly so you can hide them with tape and wallboard compound.

How to Repair Wallboard Corners

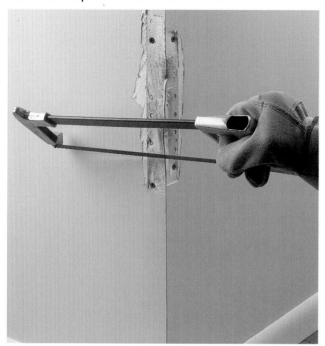

1 Drive a 1¼" wallboard screw into each flange of the metal corner bead, above and below the damaged area. Cut out the damaged section of corner bead, using a hack saw. Cut through the bead first, then the flanges, keeping the saw blade parallel to the floor. Remove the damaged section, and scrape away any loose wallboard and compound.

2 Cut a new piece of corner bead to fit exactly into the opening. Hold the replacement piece so the bead is perfectly aligned with the existing corner edge and secure it with wallboard screws. Drive the screws about ¼" from the flange edge, and alternate sides with each screw to keep the piece straight.

3 File the seams with a fine metal file to ensure a smooth transition between pieces. If you can't easily smooth the seams, cut a new replacement piece and start over.

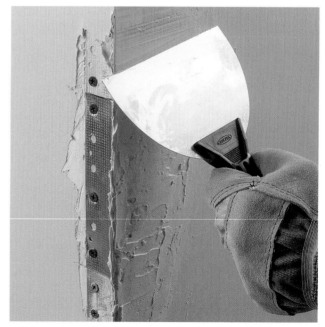

4 Hide the repair with three coats of wallboard compound, using a 6" wallboard knife. Apply the compound generously, then smooth it off with a continuous vertical stroke, letting the knife edge run along the bead. Allow the compound to dry between coats.

Repairing Plaster

Before making any repairs to a plaster wall or ceiling, check the overall condition of the area. Widespread bulging or sponginess means the plaster has pulled away from its foundation. Damaged wall plaster will remain stable for a while, but failed plaster on a ceiling is hazardous, especially if there's water damage. Call a professional to have the plaster replaced or covered with wallboard panels.

For surface repairs to plaster, and for covering joint tape, use wallboard compound. Use patching plaster for filling holes; it shrinks less than wallboard compound and is less likely to crack. Since plaster is seldom perfectly smooth, you'll have to texture the repair area to blend it in. Make the initial repair as smooth and flat as possible, to avoid the added challenge of having to hide flaws with the texture.

Everything You Need:

Tools: Scraper, paintbrush, wallboard knife.

Materials: Latex bonding liquid, patching plaster, 150-grit sandpaper.

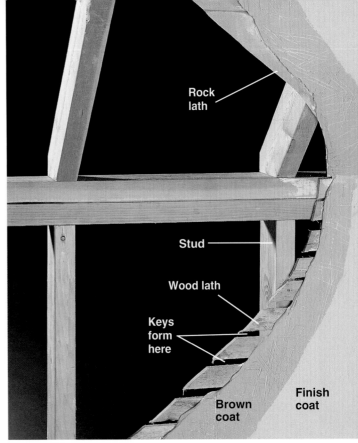

Plaster is applied in layers over a surface of wood, metal, or rock lath. When wet base plaster is pushed between strips of wood lath, it forms "keys" that hold the plaster in place. Avoid hammering a plaster wall, as the shock can disturb the surrounding surface.

How to Repair Holes in Plaster

1 Scrape or sand any texture from the area around the hole.

2 Test the edges of the hole with the scraper, and remove any loose or soft plaster.

3 Apply latex bonding liquid liberally around the edges of the hole and over the lath. Bonding liquid helps the patching plaster adhere to the wall, and it eliminates the need to moisten the surfaces with water to prevent premature drying, which causes cracking.

4 Mix the patching plaster as directed by the manufacturer, and apply it to the hole using a wallboard knife. Hold the knife almost flat, and press the plaster into the hole to force it between the lath strips and into the crevices around the edges. Leave the hole about half-full.

5 Score a crosshatch pattern in the wet plaster, to provide "tooth" for the second layer of plaster to bond with. Let the plaster dry, then apply a second coat. Smooth the patch flush with the wall, and let it dry. Sand the surface lightly with 150-grit sandpaper.

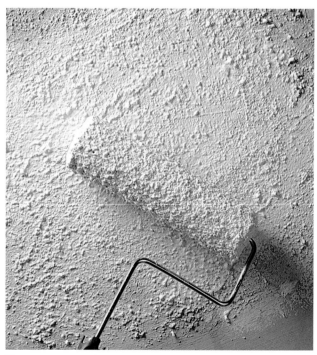

Use texture paint or wallboard compound to recreate any surface texture (page 85).

How to Repair Cracks

For cracks in plaster, scrape away any texture from the surface around the crack. Then, scrape along the crack with a bottle opener, undercutting the edges slightly. Remove any loose grit from the crack.

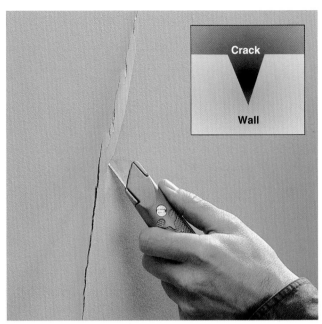

For cracks in wallboard, cut a V-groove along the crack with a utility knife. The groove should widen the crack a little, but should not go all the way through the board. If the crack runs along a seam, remove any loose joint tape, and scrape out any loose compound from the seam.

1 Fill the crack with wallboard compound, then apply a layer of compound extending about 2" on either side of the crack. Cover the crack with fiberglass wallboard joint tape, pressing it into the compound layer. Smooth the tape and remove excess compound with a 6" wallboard knife, leaving a very thin layer.

2 Apply additional coats of compound in thin layers, allowing it to dry between coats. If the repair is too thick, it will recrack. Sand the final coat with 150-grit sandpaper, then prime, paint, or texture as needed.

Texturing Walls & Ceilings

Wall and ceiling textures range from inspired art to modern monotony, and whether you've patched over the work of a gifted plasterer or scraped off a "popcorn" spray job, there's nothing more conspicuous than a big smooth spot in the middle of a textured wall. But with a little creativity, you can recreate almost any texture using texture paint or diluted wallboard compound.

Texture paints come in various thicknesses, and some contain additives, such as sand and polystyrene beads, for specific effects. Aerosol cans and hand-operated pump guns make it easy to create modern textures without special spray equipment. You can leave a texture paint as-is or apply a top coat of a different color. Like other paints, texture paints may not cover all stains, so prime the surface before you paint it.

Practice texturing on a sheet of cardboard or wallboard, and try different tools (or your hands) and material thicknesses until you find the right combination. Whatever the design, apply it carefully but with confidence; a tentative, sketchy texture job will be more noticeable than one done with bold strokes. Remember, you can always scrape it off while it's still wet and start over.

Tools & materials for texturing include: spray-on texture (1), all-purpose wallboard compound (2), texture paint (3), texture roller (4), whisk broom (5), wallboard knife (6), sponge (7), and trowel (8).

How to Texture Walls & Ceilings

Use a whisk broom for various lined patterns. Apply the texture material with a paint roller, then create the pattern with the broom.

Smooth a trowel or a wallboard knife over a partially dried texture for a "knockdown" effect.

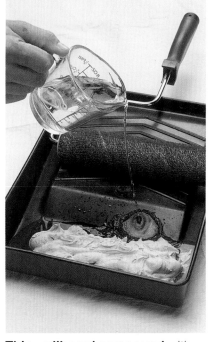

Thin wallboard compound with water, and apply it with a texture roller or any other tool.

Mending Wallcoverings

Loosened seams, bubbles, and stiff, curled edges are common wallcovering problems, all of which can be repaired with a little glue. More extensive damage, such as a puncture or tear, may call for a patch.

Most wallcoverings today are made of durable vinyl, which is shown here. If your wallcoverings are traditional paper or a specialty material, such as foil or grasscloth, check with the manufacturer for recommended repairs. Use wallpaper dough to remove stains if your wallcovering isn't washable.

If you need a patch and you don't have any wallcovering remnants in reserve, take a piece from an inconspicuous area, such as in a closet or behind an appliance or piece of furniture.

Everything You Need:

Tools: Adhesive applicator, seam roller, razor knife, sponge.

Materials: Seam adhesive, wallpaper dough, wallcovering, drafting tape.

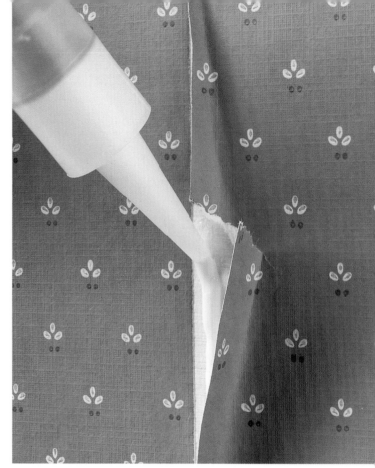

Use seam adhesive, available at wallcovering stores, for repairing vinyl wallcoverings. Check the product label for specific application and cleanup instructions.

Tips for Repairing Wallcovering

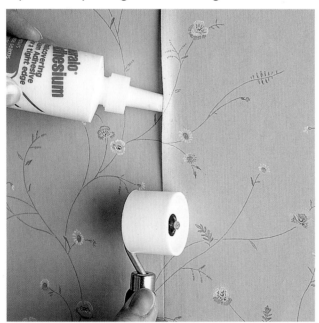

To fix seams and curled edges, lift the edge of the wallcovering and insert the tip of a glue applicator. Squirt adhesive onto the wall. Press the edge back in place with a seam roller, and wipe away excess adhesive with a damp sponge. If the edges are stiff and won't lie flat, soften the wallcovering by rubbing it with a damp sponge periodically for 20 or 30 minutes. Let it dry partially before applying the glue.

Clean soiled wallcovering with wallpaper dough or a gum eraser, available at wallcovering stores and decorating and home centers. As the dough becomes soiled, fold it into itself to expose a clean surface.

How to Fix a Bubble

1 Cut a slit through the bubble using a sharp razor knife. If there is a pattern in the wallcovering, cut along a line to hide the slit.

2 Insert the tip of a glue applicator through the slit and apply adhesive sparingly to the wall under the wallcovering.

3 Press the wallcovering gently to rebond it. Use a clean damp sponge to press the flap down and wipe away excess glue.

How to Patch Wallcovering

1 Fasten a scrap of matching wallcovering over the damaged portion with drafting tape, aligning the patch so the patterns match exactly.

2 Holding a razor knife blade at a 90° angle to the wall, cut through both layers of wallcovering (but not into the wallboard). If the wallcovering has strong pattern lines, cut along the lines to hide the seams. With less definite patterns, cut irregular lines.

3 Remove the scrap and patch, then peel away the damaged wallcovering. Apply adhesive to the back of the patch and position it in the hole so that the patterns match. Rinse the area with a clean, damp sponge.

Remove broken tiles carefully. Start by removing the grout from around the tile (page 89). Then, use a cold chisel and a hammer to break the tile into small pieces. Always drive the chisel inward to avoid damaging neighboring tiles. After you've removed the tile, scrape the old adhesive from the wall.

Everything You Need:

Tools: Awl, utility knife, grout saw, grout brush, cold chisel, hammer, scraper, rubber grout float, sponge, razor blade.

Materials: Tile, tile adhesive, grout, rubbing alcohol, silicone caulk, grout sealer.

Repairing Ceramic Tile Walls & Ceilings

Most tile surfaces are impervious to water, but the grout between tiles can wash away over the years, leaving narrow gaps that allow water to reach the wall surface and cause further damage. Where tile meets other elements, such as a tub, shower stall, or countertop, caulk creates the necessary watertight seal. But caulk, too, deteriorates over time, becoming hard and losing its grip. Cracks in tile—even fine cracks—also permit water penetration.

Minor tile repairs are easy and worthwhile. It takes only a few minutes to recaulk an old joint and a few minutes more to replace a cracked or broken tile. Regrouting a tiled wall or ceiling is not so easy, but sometimes it's the only way to save your tile–and a lot of money. However, if the tile is spongy or sounds hollow when you tap on it, have a professional check it out: it may be too far gone for regrouting to help.

Ask a tile retailer about grout colors. And whether your grout is new or old, apply a grout sealer to protect it from stains and water damage.

How to Replace a Broken Tile

1 Remove the tile (see above). Test-fit the new tile to be sure it sits flush with the surrounding tile. Spread ceramic tile adhesive on the back of the new tile, then set it in place and twist it slightly to create a good bond.

2 When the adhesive has dried, apply premixed grout with a sponge or grout float (page 89). Let the grout set for 10-15 minutes, then wipe away excess with a damp sponge.

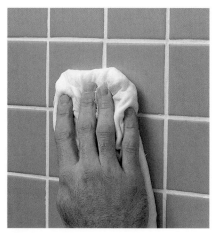

3 Let the grout dry for about 1 hour, then polish the tile with a clean dry cloth to remove the powdery residue.

How to Recaulk Around a Bathtub or Shower Stall

1 Cut and scrape out the old caulk with an awl or utility knife; use a razor blade on flat surfaces. Clean the joint with rubbing alcohol and a cloth.

2 Fill the tub with water so it will pull away from the tile, then fill the joint with a quality silicone caulk. Apply just enough to fill the gap and seal to the edge of the tile.

3 Smooth the caulk into a cove shape with a wet fingertip. Wipe up any mess with a clean cloth. Let the caulk dry completely before draining or using the tub.

How to Regrout Tiles

1 Scrape out the old grout completely, using an awl, a utility knife, or a grout saw (or all three). Brush out the joints with a grout brush. Mix the grout according to the manufacturer's directions, but mix only enough for one section, as the grout dries quickly.

2 Spread the grout liberally over the tiles, using a rubber grout float. Then, work the grout well into joints by holding the float face at a 60° angle to the tile and dragging it forcefully over the tiles at a 45° angle to the joints. Let the grout set for 10-15 minutes, then wipe away excess with a damp sponge, rinsing the sponge frequently.

3 Let the grout dry for about 1 hour, then wipe away the powdery residue from the tile faces with a soft, dry cloth. Apply caulk around a bathtub or shower stall (above). Do not use the tub or shower for 24 hours. Seal the grout after it has fully cured (check manufacturer's instructions).

Floors & Stairs

Repairing Floors

Your home probably has several different types of floor covering, each with its own maintenance and repair needs. The most important aspect of maintaining any type of flooring is regular cleaning. Why? Because dirt is not only unsightly, it's abrasive. It dulls and scratches smooth floor finishes, and it stains and tears carpet fibers. Ask the manufacturer or supplier of your floor covering for cleaning tips and advice about compatible and effective cleaning products.

One common flooring complaint involves squeaking, common because squeaks occur in the wood structure, which changes with the seasons (hardwood floors are the worst offenders). But with a few simple tricks, you can reduce or even eliminate most floor squeaks.

Floor repairs are easiest if you have some extra material on hand. Spare tiles, carpet remnants, and leftover boards are perfect for patches and other extensive repairs. If you don't have a reserve, remove patch material from an inconspicuous area, such as in a closet or under an appliance. Be sure to replace "borrowed" material wherever water damage is a concern.

While surface repairs for wood floors and carpet typically are for appearance, repairs on vinyl-

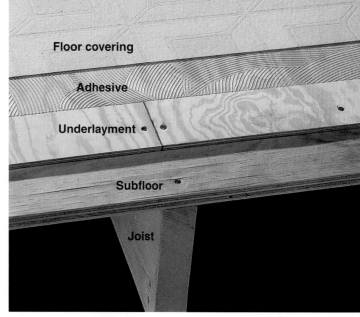

Floors are supported by heavy framing members, called *joists*, and a plywood or 1 × 6 *subfloor*. Vinyl and tile floor coverings are bonded to an *underlayment*, while carpet and hardwood planks are typically laid over the subfloor.

and tile-covered floors are necessary to maintain a protective moisture barrier. If water is allowed beneath the surface, it can destroy the adhesive layer that holds the floor covering down, resulting in damage to the wood structure.

A staircase is another floor surface that shows signs of wear: squeaky steps, loose railings, and damaged balusters are the most common problems. With stairs, however, safety is an added concern. Be sure the railings are sturdy and well attached and the balusters are in good condition.

Tools for floor repairs include: cold chisel (1), J-roller (2), rubber grout float (3), knee kicker (4), notched trowels (5), heat gun (6), subfloor fastening device (7), and grout saw (8).

Silencing Squeaky Floors

Floor squeaks are caused by loose floorboards rubbing together, by gaps between the subfloor and joists, or by any of the wood elements rubbing against a nail. The two options for relief, then, are lubricating the boards or adding fasteners or wedges to reduce movement.

If you have access to the underside of the floor, you can make the repairs without needing to hide them. Locating noisy boards can be tough, so have a friend walk around as you investigate from below. You can also chart the squeaks by measuring from elements common to both sides, such as pipes or heating ducts.

Everything You Need:

Tools: Toothbrush, drill, hammer.

Materials: Lubricant, wood screws, hardwood shims, wood glue, floor fastening system.

Lubricate hardwood floor boards with talcum powder, mineral oil, powdered graphite, or dance floor wax. Work the lubricant between the boards with a cloth or a toothbrush, then bounce on the floor to distribute the lubricant.

Tips for Eliminating Squeaks

Drive wood screws to draw hardwood flooring to the subfloor. Drill pilot holes for the screws, and make sure the screws are not long enough to poke through the tops of the floorboards.

Use thin hardwood shims to fill gaps between the subfloor and the joists. Dab some wood glue on a shim and tap it into place, just until it's snug.

Fasten subfloors through carpet using a special device available at floor stores. After driving the special screws with a scored shank, break off the end, just below the surface of the subfloor.

Renewing Hardwood Floors

Renewing your hardwood floor may require no more than a thorough cleaning, although common repairs include patching and replacing floorboards. Before making any repairs to a hardwood floor, find out what type of finish the floor carries. This is important because you may need to refinish a repaired area to protect the wood and to blend it in with the existing floorboards.

Start your investigation by feeling the wood. Natural, or *penetrating*, finishes soak into the wood, leaving a grained texture; these usually have a protective coating of wax. *Surface* finishes seal over the grain, forming a smooth layer. The most common surface finish today is polyurethane, which has a plastic-like appearance. Conduct a solvent test (right) to determine what type of surface finish you have.

Because both wood and finishes change color with age, you'll need to color any new or sanded wood with wood restorer or stain to match the old boards. Start with some test pieces, and apply stain and the appropriate finish. Wait a day or more, then compare the colors with the floor.

Identify surface finishes using solvents. In an inconspicuous area, rub in different solvents to see if the finish dissolves, softens, or is removed. Denatured alcohol removes shellac; lacquer thinner removes lacquer. If neither of those work, try nail polish remover containing acetone; this removes varnish but it won't remove polyurethane.

Everything You Need:

Tools: Vacuum, brush or nylon pad, buffing machine (optional), putty knife, drill, circular saw, chisel, hammer, caulk gun, nail set, paintbrush.

Materials: Solvents, paste wax, tinted wood patch, sandpaper, stain, construction adhesive, spiral shanked flooring nails, floor finish.

How to Clean & Renew Waxed Hardwood Floors

1 Vacuum the entire floor to remove grit and dirt. A vacuum with a sweeper attachment works better than a broom.

2 Remove dirty, built-up wax with hot water and mild dishwashing detergent and a brush or nylon pad. Or, use a commercial wood floor cleaner. Work in small sections, wiping up any water and wax before moving to the next section.

3 When the floor is dry, apply a quality floor wax. Paste wax is more difficult to apply than liquid, but it lasts much longer. For an even, polished finish, buff the floor with a rented buffing machine.

How to Patch Hardwood Floors

1 Use latex wood patch to fill in deep scratches, gouges and nail holes. Select a tinted patch that matches the color of your floor, and press it into the hole with a putty knife. Smooth the patch flat and remove any excess at the edges.

2 Allow the patch to dry, then sand it flush with the surface, using fine-grit sandpaper. Sand in the direction of the wood grain.

3 If necessary, blend in the area with stain or wood restorer. Apply wax or the appropriate surface finish (page 95).

How to Replace Damaged Floor Boards

1 Drill overlapping holes at the ends of damaged boards, using a spade bit. For long boards, draw a square cutting line beyond the damage and mark it with tape (see step 3). Set the depth of a circular saw to cut the exact thickness of the hardwood, then make several cuts between the holes.

2 Chisel out the center of the cutout, working toward the edges. Don't pry or drive the chisel against undamaged boards.

3 To complete a cut in the middle of a board, square off the edge at the cutting line, using a sharp, wide chisel.

How to Replace Damaged Floor Boards (continued)

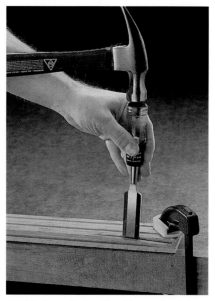

4 Select replacement boards of matching size, color, and grain, and cut them to fit. Install the boards one at a time, using construction adhesive and spiral-shanked flooring nails. Drill pilot holes, and drive the nails at a 45° angle through the base of the tongue and into the subfloor. Whenever possible, nail into joists. Set the nails with a nail set.

5 To install the final board, chisel off the lower lip of the groove. Also remove the tongue on the end, if necessary. Apply adhesive to the board, and set it in place.

6 Drill pilot holes at the ends of the final board and along the groove side, about every 8-12". Drive flooring nails through the pilot holes, then set the nails and fill the holes with tinted wood putty. Stain and finish the boards as needed to protect them and blend them into the surrounding area (see below).

How to Touch-up a Surface Finish on New or Patched Boards

1 Determine what type of surface finish is on the floor (page 93). Test stain on scrap pieces until the color matches the existing boards. For patches, conduct these tests in an inconspicuous area. Apply a finish to the test pieces and let them dry for 1-3 days, to see if the color remains consistent.

2 Lightly sand the edges of the surrounding boards, using fine-grit sandpaper to roughen the surface so the new finish will bond to it. Clean the area with a cloth dipped in mineral spirits, then stain the new boards and let them dry.

3 Apply two coats of finish to the new boards, following the manufacturer's instructions. Apply a third coat over the new and sanded areas to "feather" the new finish into the old. (If the old finish is polyurethane, use oil-based polyurethane for the touch-up).

Fixing Carpet Problems

Your carpet's greatest enemies are dirt and stains. Dirt is unattractive; it also abrades carpet fibers, causing premature wear. Stains look bad, of course, but the bigger problem is that they attract dirt.

For everyday spills, follow the cleaning tips given here, using a cleaner or a household solution given in the chart below. For persistent stains or stains of mysterious origins, use a commercial carpet stain remover or a dry-cleaning solvent.

Be sure to test any cleaning solution before using it on your carpet. Apply the solution to an inconspicuous area and let it sit for about a minute. Blot the carpet with a white paper towel to check for color bleeding, then inspect the carpet fibers for damage or excessive residue.

You can cut shallow burns from plush carpet fibers using small scissors. Do not cut berber or other loop pile carpet, however, because the pile is created with a continuous yarn.

For some repairs, you may need to rent tools, such as a knee-kicker, from a carpet store.

Use a large spoon to pick up spills. Spoons capture liquids well without damaging fibers. Scoop toward the center of the stain to avoid spreading.

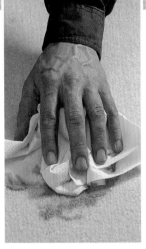

Do not rub stains—blot them. Apply cleaning solution to a cloth or paper towel, then blot the stain, working from the outside toward the center to avoid spreading the stain.

Everything You Need:

Tools: Spoon, cookie-cutter tool, knee kicker, wallboard knife.

Materials: Paper towels, cleaning solution, double-face carpet tape, seam adhesive.

Remedies for Carpet Stains

Find the type of spill in the chart below, then apply each solution or cleaning agent in the order given, blotting the area dry between applications. Use the following proportions to mix the basic solutions:

Basic solutions:
A: 1 tablespoon ammonia, ½ cup water
D: Detergent (liquid dish or fine-fabric), diluted with water
V: ⅓ cup vinegar, ⅔ cup water

Blood, fresh: Apply cold water or club soda and blot dry; D
   dried: D
Catsup: D; A; D
Candle wax, Crayon: Cover stain w/ ice pack, then scrape off brittle wax or crayon; next, cover stain w/ paper towel, then heat w/ iron: wax should melt and be absorbed by towel; apply commercial cleaner
Chewing gum: Cover stain w/ ice pack, then scrape off brittle gum; apply commercial cleaner
Chocolate: D; A

Coffee, Cola: D; V
Feces: D; A; V
Fruit juice: D; A; V
Furniture polish: Apply commercial cleaner or dry-cleaning solvent; D
Gravy: D; A; D
Grease: May require solvent cleaner to break down grease; D
Ice cream: D; A; V
Lipstick: Apply commercial cleaner; D; A; V
Paint, Latex, wet: D
   dried: Apply water-soluble paint & varnish remover (test first); D; V (1:10 solution)

Paint, Oil (alkyd): Blot w/ paint thinner, turpentine, or commercial cleaner
Shoe polish: Apply commercial cleaner or paint thinner; D; A; V
Soot: Sprinkle area with salt and let sit for 15 mins., then vacuum without rubbing the pile (to avoid spreading)
Tea: D; V
Urine: V; A; V; D
Wine: D; V; D

How to Patch Damaged Carpet

1 Cut out extensive damage, using a cookie-cutter tool. Press the cutter down and twist to cut away the carpet.

2 Cut a replacement patch from scrap carpeting, using the cookie cutter. Insert double-face carpet tape under the carpet so that tape overlaps the patch seam.

3 Press the patch into place. Make sure the direction of the nap or pattern matches the existing carpet. Seal the seam with seam adhesive to prevent unraveling.

How to Restretch Loose Carpet

1 Turn the knob on the head of a knee kicker to adjust the depth of the prongs: they should extend far enough to grab the carpet backing without penetrating the padding. Starting from a corner or near a point where the carpet is firmly attached, press the kicker head into the carpet, about 2" from the wall.

2 Thrust your knee into the cushion of the kicker to force the carpet toward the wall. Then, use a wallboard knife to tuck the carpet down behind the tackless strip so the backing grabs the points on the strip. If the carpet is still loose, trim the edge with a utility knife, and stretch it again.

Repairing Vinyl Floor Coverings

The most common types of vinyl flooring are sheet and tile. Sheet flooring is more prone to gouges, tears, and scratches, while tiles tend to buckle, crack, or come loose. Since vinyl floor coverings are typically used for wet areas, such as bathrooms, kitchens, and utility rooms, you should make repairs as soon as possible to prevent water from causing further damage.

Use seam sealer to repair bubbles and minor scratches in sheet vinyl. For deeper damage, make a patch by employing the double-cutting technique used for hanging wallcovering. Damaged vinyl tiles are easy to replace, provided you have replacement tile available. If necessary, remove tile from a hidden area to use as patch material.

Repair bubbles in sheet vinyl, using seam sealer. Cut a small slit through the vinyl in the center of the bubble, using a sharp utility knife. Insert the tip of the sealer container, or use a glue syringe, and squirt a small amount of sealer under the vinyl. Press the bubble flat with a roller, and wipe up excess sealer. Cover the repair with a flat board and weights to keep it flat while the adhesive dries.

Everything You Need:

Tools: Utility knife, roller, framing square, washable marker, putty knife, heat gun, notched trowel.

Materials: Seam sealer, board, mineral spirits, replacement vinyl, tape, vinyl adhesive.

Remove tough stains, such as asphalt, with mineral spirits or household bleach. Wet a rag with the solution, and place it over the stain. Lay a plastic bag over the rag to slow evaporation. Wait 1-2 hours, then wipe up the stain. **Always test solvents** in an inconspicuous area before using them elsewhere on the floor.

How to Patch Sheet Vinyl

1 Select scrap vinyl that matches the existing flooring. Place the scrap over the damaged area and adjust it until the pattern matches. Tape the patch to the floor.

2 Use a framing square and a washable marker to outline the patch. If possible, draw along pattern lines to conceal the patch seams. Use a utility knife to cut through both layers of vinyl, then remove the damaged vinyl with a putty knife.

3 Apply mineral spirits to dissolve the old adhesive, then scrape the surface clean with a putty knife. Apply new vinyl adhesive to the patch, then fit it into the hole. Use a roller to smooth and bond the patch, then wipe away excess adhesive. Seal the edges of the patch with seam sealer.

How to Replace Vinyl Floor Tiles

1 Use a heat gun to heat the tile and soften the underlying adhesive. Be careful not to melt the tile. Lift out the tile with a putty knife. If you don't have a heat gun, set a pan of ice cubes over the tile to make the adhesive brittle, allowing the tile to pop up easily.

2 Apply mineral spirits to dissolve the adhesive, then scrape away the adhesive with a putty knife.

3 Apply vinyl tile adhesive to the underlayment, using a notched trowel. Set the tile in place, press it firmly with a roller to ensure a good bond, then wipe away excess adhesive. Let the repair area dry undisturbed.

Repairing Ceramic Tile Floors

Like the tile on your bathroom or kitchen walls, floor tile must be watertight. All the grout lines must be solid and full, and every tile must be free of cracks or chips. Neglecting problems can result in damage to the underlayment and subfloor, and possibly to the entire tile job.

Perhaps the greatest challenge with tile repair is matching the grout color. If you're regrouting an entire floor, just select a color that compliments the tile; if you're replacing a tile, you have to blend the new grout with the old. A good tile dealer can help you get the best color match.

Floor tile is typically bonded to the floor with a cement-based adhesive, known as *thin-set mortar.* If you find another adhesive, such as mastic, under the original tile, use the same type to install replacement tiles.

Apply grout sealer to grout joints every 1-2 years to protect against water, wear, and stains. Use a sponge brush to spread the sealer and keep it off the tiles. Allow new grout to cure fully before sealing it.

Everything You Need:

Tools: Sponge brush, utility knife, grout saw or rotary tool, cold chisel, hammer, putty knife, notched trowel, rubber mallet, screwdriver, rounded sponge, rubber grout float.

Materials: Grout sealer, thin-set mortar, 2 × 4, carpet, grout.

How to Regrout a Tiled Floor

1 Completely remove the old grout, using a rotary tool, utility knife (and several blades), or a grout saw. Spread the new grout liberally over the tiles, using a rubber grout float. Force grout into the joints, holding the float almost flat, then drag the float across the joints diagonally, tilting the face at a 45° angle.

2 Remove excess grout by making a second pass with the float. Work diagonally across the joint lines, and tilt the float at a steep angle to the tile faces.

3 Let the grout set for 10-15 minutes, then wipe away excess with a damp sponge, rinsing frequently. Fill in low spots by applying and smoothing extra grout with your finger. Let the grout dry for about 1 hour, then polish the tile faces with a dry cloth to remove the powdery residue. Seal the grout after it cures completely.

How to Replace a Floor Tile

1 Remove the grout from around the damaged tile, using a rotary tool, utility knife (and several blades), or a grout saw. Then, carefully break apart the tile, using a cold chisel and hammer.

2 Scrape away the old adhesive with a putty knife. Make sure the base surface is smooth and flat.

3 Use a notched trowel to cover the entire back of the replacement tile with an even layer of thin-set mortar.

4 Set the tile in place, and press down firmly to create a good bond. If necessary, use a carpet-covered 2×4 and a rubber mallet to tap the tile flush with the neighboring tiles.

5 Use a small screwdriver to re-move excess mortar that has oozed into the grout joints, then wipe up any mortar from the tile surface. When the mortar has dried completely, grout around the tile (page 100).

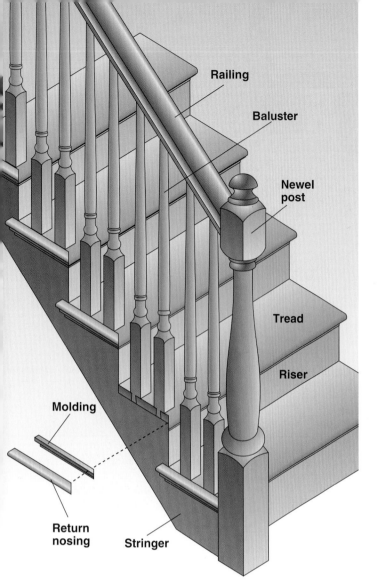

Railing

Baluster

Newel post

Tread

Riser

Molding

Return nosing

Stringer

A staircase starts with two or more *stringers*, which support the *tread* and *riser* of each step. The *balusters* shown here attach to the treads with dovetailed joints concealed by *return nosing* and molding pieces.

Fixing a Staircase

Aside from squeaks and loose railings, there's not much that can go wrong with a staircase. Like floors, stairs squeak when the lumber becomes warped or when loose boards rub against nails or each other. Eliminating squeaks is easiest if you have access to the underside of the staircase. If not, you can work on noisy steps from above, provided there's no carpet in the way.

Loose railings are shabby and unsafe. With freestanding railings, which are supported by solid or hollow *newel posts* at the ends of the staircase and at the landings, the problem may lie in the newels' structural connections or in the railing's connection with the newels. Wall-mounted railings are supported by brackets with screws driven into wall studs. If these come loose, tighten the screws, or install longer screws to increase their holding power.

Balusters, the vertical spindles that stand between the steps and the railing, do little to prevent horizontal sway, but a broken baluster is unattractive and can be dangerous, especially for children. You can replace a baluster with a stock piece from a lumber yard or have a woodturner create a custom duplicate for you.

Everything You Need:

Tools: Drill, hammer, utility knife, nail set, ratchet wrench, pry bar, saw, pipe wrench, T-bevel.

Materials: Wood blocks, construction adhesive, screws, shims, wood glue, wood putty or plugs, quarter-round molding, finish nails, sandpaper, string, wood dowel, lag screw.

How to Stop Squeaks from Below

Glue wood blocks to the joints between the treads and risers with construction adhesive. Once the blocks are in place, drill pilot holes and fasten the blocks to the treads and risers with screws. Don't use the repaired steps until the adhesive has dried.

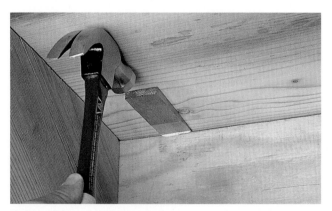

Drive shims into gaps between treads and risers. Apply wood glue to thin hardwood shims and tap them in place just until they're snug. Let the glue dry before using the steps.

How to Stop Squeaks from Above

Drill pilot holes and drive screws down through stair treads and into risers. Sink the screws below the surface and fill the holes with wood putty or wood plugs.

Tap glued shims under loose treads. Use a block to prevent splitting, and drive the shim just until it's snug. When the gluc has dried, cut the shim flush with the riser, using a utility knife.

Use quarter-round molding to reinforce the joints between treads and risers. Drill pilot holes, and drive finish nails into the riser and tread. Set the nails with a nail set.

How to Tighten Railings

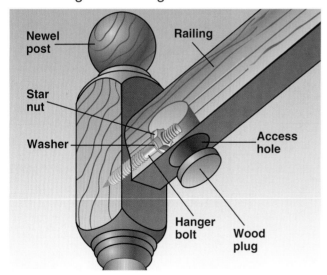

Newel post

Railing

Star nut

Washer

Access hole

Hanger bolt

Wood plug

Railings connect to newel posts (and to other railing sections) with internal hanger bolts. Each bolt has a coarse-threaded end that is driven into the post, and a machine-threaded end that fits into a hole in the end of the railing. The wood parts are drawn together by a *star nut* that is tightened through an access hole on the underside of the railing.

To tighten a loose connection, drill out the access hole plug, then loosen the nut a little by using a small wrench or by tapping the points of the star nut with a nail set and hammer. Scrape or sand the old glue from the joint. Apply a thin layer of wood glue to the mating surfaces, using a string to spread the glue. Tighten the star nut to close the joint. When the glue has dried, cut a new plug from a wood dowel and glue it in place. Sand the plug flush with the surface.

How to Tighten a Solid Newel Post

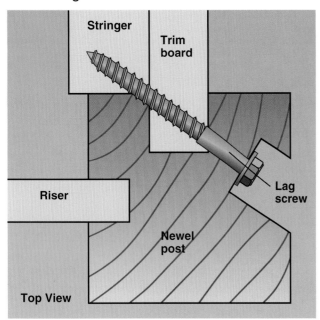

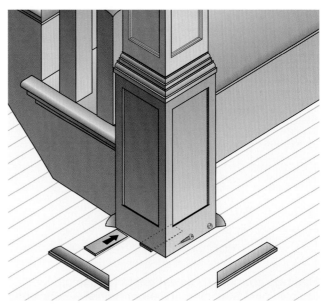

Solid wood newel posts are bolted or screwed to the floor, a stair tread or riser, a stringer, or even a joist underneath the floor. Like the hanger bolt in the railing, these fasteners may be concealed by wood plugs (page 103). Remove the plug and tighten the fasteners if possible. If you can't find any fasteners to tighten or if they are inaccessible, drive a new lag screw to secure the loose newel to the stair stringer.

Using a ¾" spade bit, drill a counterbore into the post, about ¾" deep. Aim the hole toward the stringer. Drill a ⁷⁄₃₂"-dia. pilot hole through the center of the counterbore and into the stringer. Then, widen the pilot hole through the post only, using a ⁵⁄₁₆" bit; this prevents the screw from splitting the wood. Fit a washer on a ⁵⁄₁₆"-dia × 4"-long lag screw and drive the screw with a ratchet wrench, but don't overtighten it. Plug the counterbore with a glued piece of wood dowel.

How to Tighten a Hollow Newel Post

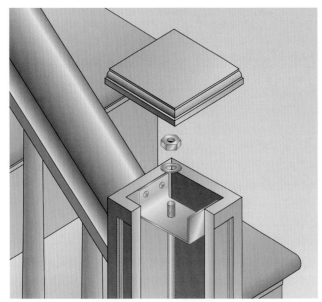

Hollow newel posts may be fastened in a variety of ways. If your newel has a cap on top, start your investigation there. Pry off the cap, and look inside the post for a nut at the end of a threaded rod. Tighten this nut to stabilize the post. If there's no cap, check around the base for moldings that may conceal fasteners, or look for a nut from underneath the floor.

Drive thin, tapered shims under all accessible sides of the base to stabilize a newel post when you can't reach any fasteners. Remove any base molding first, then use a hammer to tap the shims in incrementally, alternating sides to ensure the post stands straight. Or, drive screws at an angle into the floor. Replace the molding to conceal the shims or screw heads.

How to Replace a Baluster

1 Look underneath the railing to see if there are wood spacers (called *fillets)*, between the top ends of the balusters (see step 4). Remove the fillet directly above the damaged baluster, then cut the baluster in half with a reciprocating saw or handsaw. Make the cut in a plain section of the baluster, leaving intact any details needed for finding a replacement. Pull the top half of the baluster from the railing.

2 If the baluster base rests on a solid section of tread, it should have a dowel end that's glued into a hole in the tread. Break the joint by twisting the baluster with a pipe wrench. Ream the hole with a spade bit if there's any stuck wood. If the base sits on a seam where a piece of trim (called *return nosing*) covers the end of the tread, the baluster is probably secured with a square tenon or dovetail joint (see page 102). Remove the trim and carefully knock the tenon or dovetail pin from the groove.

3 Measure between the tread and railing, and cut the replacement baluster to fit. Use a T-bevel or the old baluster to find the proper angle for the top end. Apply wood glue to all mating surfaces at both ends, and install the new baluster.

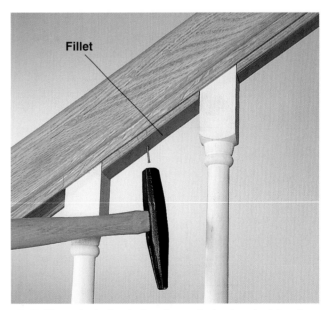

Fillet

4 Drill angled pilot holes through the back side of the baluster, near the top end, and into the railing, then secure the baluster with finish nails. Glue and nail the fillet back in place. Replace any trim, set all the nails, and fill the nail holes with wood putty.

Heating, Ventilation &
Air Conditioning Systems

Repairing HVAC Systems

Heating, ventilation, and air conditioning systems are often referred to as a group by the term *HVAC*. This is because they share a common purpose: to keep the air in your home clean and comfortable. All HVAC systems—even older hot-water-based systems—rely on the flow of air to heat, cool, and ventilate your home. The health of your HVAC systems directly affects the quality of the indoor air you breathe.

That's why it's important to keep your HVAC systems in good condition by replacing filters, checking burners, cleaning fans and vents, and so on. It's also a good idea to periodically have a technician inspect flues, ducts, vents, chimneys, and your HVAC equipment for leaks and other potential problems.

HVAC repairs that you can do yourself typically involve seasonal inspection and maintenance. These tasks help you become familiar with your HVAC systems, and make it much easier to keep your equipment running efficiently.

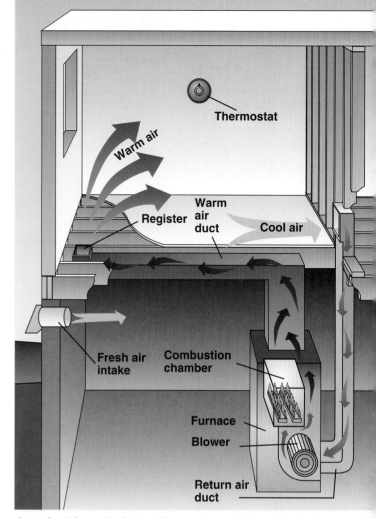

A typical forced air heating system delivers heated air to a room through registers while drawing cool air through return ducts. The cool air is reheated in the furnace and recirculated for maximum efficiency. A fresh air intake provides a constant supply of healthy outdoor air.

Tools for HVAC repairs include: neon circuit tester (1), funnel (2), multi-tester (3), all-purpose household oil (4), pipe wrench (5), bucket (6), hose (7), open-end wrenches (8), pocket thermometer (9), screwdrivers (10), ratchet wrench (11), nut drivers (12), fin comb (13), chisel (14), broad-billed pliers (15), and pilot jet tool (16).

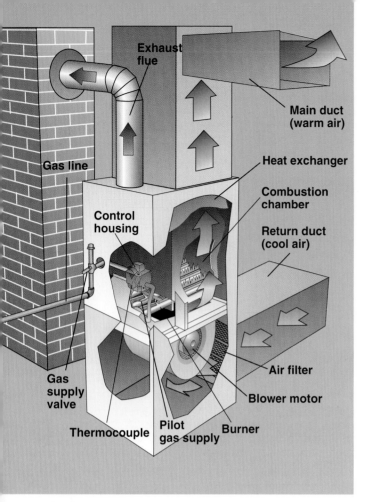

Exhaust flue

Main duct (warm air)

Gas line

Heat exchanger

Control housing

Combustion chamber

Return duct (cool air)

Gas supply valve

Air filter

Blower motor

Thermocouple

Pilot gas supply

Burner

Routine inspection of the main components and regular filter cleaning or replacement will maximize your furnace's efficiency and keep your indoor air clean.

How to Balance the Air Supply

LIVING ROOM

SUMMER

WINTER

Damper handle

Adjust the dampers in individual ducts to balance the flow of air throughout the house. Rooms farthest from the furnace need the most air, and vice versa. After each adjustment, wait a few hours for the air temperature to stabilize. Mark the room and setting for each damper. If you have central air conditioning, balance the air flow in the fall and again in the spring.

Repairing a Gas Furnace

Whether it's old or new, a gas furnace (left) has three main power systems—the blower, the pilot (or igniter), and the burners. Specific devices have changed over the years, but the general operation is the same: when the house temperature drops, the thermostat sends a signal to start the burners, which are ignited by the pilot or other type of igniter. In the combustion chamber, the burners heat up the surrounding air, which then flows into the heat exchanger, while waste gases are vented to the chimney. The blower circulates cool air past the heat exchanger and into the main duct. From there, the hot air branches off along the network of ducts to heat the different rooms of the house.

If your furnace is older, it probably has a *standing pilot*—a small, constant gas flame. It is equipped with a safety device, known as a *thermocouple*, which has a metal tip that sits directly in the pilot flame and shuts off the gas if the flame goes out. If your furnace won't start, check the pilot: most likely, the flame has gone out. Just follow the directions on the control housing or the furnace access cover to relight the pilot.

If the furnace squeaks and rumbles as it runs, it's probably time to tune up the blower motor. Even if everything seems to be running smoothly, it's important to check the pilot, blower, and burners before each heating season.

A newer furnace may have one of several types of electronic pilots that use an intermittent flame or spark, or it may have a hot-surface igniter with an electric element that heats up to ignite the burner flame. Some models also have a computerized control center to monitor important functions for maximum efficiency and safety. See page 112 for tips on maintaining an electronic ignition furnace.

See page 112 for tips on maintaining an electronic ignition furnace.

Everything You Need:

Tools: Open-end wrenches, ratchet wrench, straightedge, screwdrivers, nut drivers, pilot jet tool, pocket thermometer.

Materials: All-purpose household oil.

How to Repair a Furnace Blower Motor

1 Shut off power to the furnace at the main service panel (page 33). Remove the access panel to the blower housing, and inspect the motor. Some motors have oil ports and an adjustable belt; others are self-lubricating and have a direct-drive mechanism. Wipe the motor clean with a dry cloth.

2 Look for oil fill ports (the access panel may have a diagram showing their locations). Remove the port covers, if there are any, and add a few drops of all-purpose oil. Reattach the covers.

3 Hold a straightedge flush with the flat sides of the motor and blower pulleys to make sure they are properly aligned with each other.

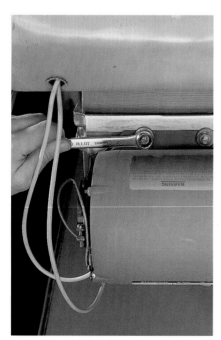  

4 To align the pulleys, loosen the mounting bolts on the motor's sliding bracket. Move the motor sideways until the pulleys are aligned, then tighten the bolts.

5 Check the drive belt tension by pressing down on the belt midway between the pulleys: it should flex about 1". Replace the belt if it is cracked, worn, or brittle.

6 To adjust the belt tension, turn the adjustment bolt, located on the motor housing or mounting bracket. Replace the access panel before restoring the power.

How to Inspect the Pilot & Thermocouple

1 Check a standing pilot light before the start of each season. If you can't see the pilot clearly, shut off the pilot gas supply by turning the knob on the control housing. Wait 10 minutes, then remove the pilot cover. Relight the pilot following the directions on the control housing or the furnace access panel.

2 Inspect the pilot flame. A weak flame (left) will be blue and will just touch the tip of the thermocouple. A flame that's too strong (center) will also be blue but may be noisy and extend beyond the thermocouple. A proper flame (right) will have a yellow tip and cover about ½" of the thermocouple.

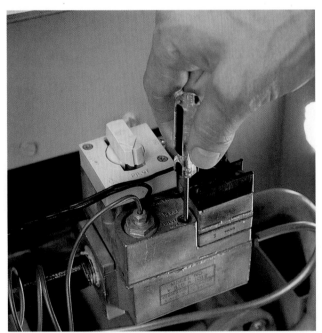

3 Adjust the pilot flame by turning the adjustment screw on the control housing. If the flame appears weak after adjustment, remove the pilot housing, and clean the pilot jet (page 111). If the pilot won't stay lit, and you know the gas supply is sufficient, replace the thermocouple (step 4).

4 Shut off power to the furnace at the main service panel, and turn off the gas supply. Use an open-end wrench to loosen the thermocouple tube fitting from the control housing or gas valve. Unscrew the thermocouple from the pilot housing and install a new one. Restore the power and gas. Light the pilot and inspect the flame to make sure the thermocouple is positioned properly.

How to Clean & Adjust the Pilot Light

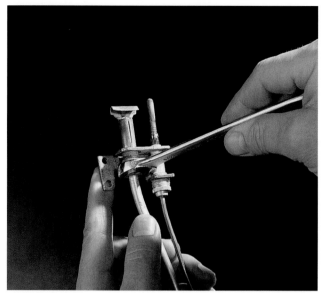

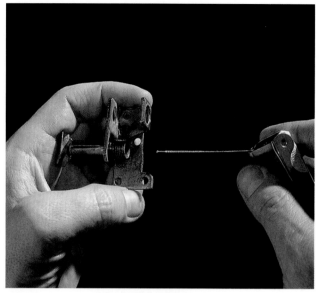

1 Shut off power to the furnace at the main service panel, and turn off the gas supply, including the pilot gas supply, if your unit has a separate one. Wait 30 minutes for the parts to cool. Use two open-end wrenches to remove the pilot gas tube from the control housing. Remove the thermocouple from the control housing, then unscrew the pilot housing; remove the pilot gas line and thermocouple.

2 Clean the pilot jet, or orifice, in the pilot housing with a pilot jet tool. Be careful not to scratch or enlarge the orifice. Reattach the pilot gas line and thermocouple to the pilot housing and install the housing. Reattach the gas line and thermocouple to the control housing. Restore the power and gas supply. Light the pilot, and adjust the flame, if necessary.

How to Inspect & Adjust the Burner Flame

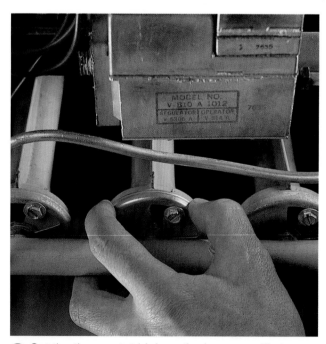

1 The color of the burner flame will tell you if the burner is getting the right mixture of gas and air. The flame should be blue, with a bluish-green flame at the center and occasional streaks of yellow (top). If the flame appears too blue or too yellow, adjust the air shutter at the end of the burner tube.

2 Set the thermostat high so the burners will stay on. Loosen the air shutter locking screw on the end of the burner tube. Open the shutter wide, then close it slowly until the flame's color is right (you may want to wear gloves for this). Tighten the locking screw, adjust the remaining burners, and then reset the thermostat. If your shutters aren't adjustable, call a professional for service.

Tips for Servicing an Electronic Ignition Furnace

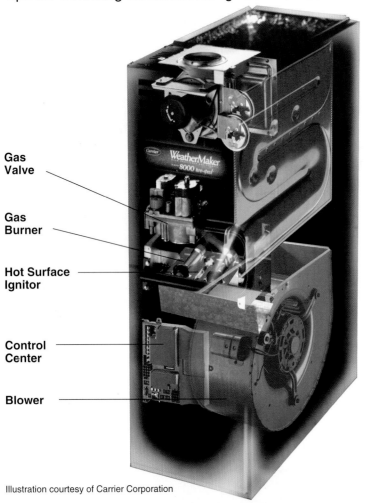

Gas Valve

Gas Burner

Hot Surface Ignitor

Control Center

Blower

Illustration courtesy of Carrier Corporation

Compare the temperature in the air supply duct to the temperature in the return duct. With some furnaces, the difference in temperature must stay within a specific range to avoid damaging the furnace (check your owner's manual). Insert a pocket thermometer into the duct expansion joints to determine the temperature.

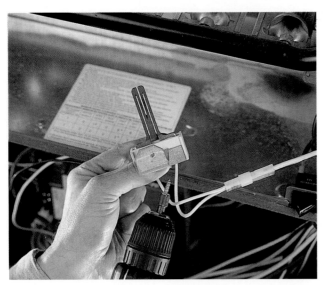

A hot-surface igniter is used to light the burners on some furnaces. The igniter should be located just beyond the ignition end of the burner tubes. Replace a faulty igniter by removing the mounting screw and disconnecting the igniter wires. Make sure the replacement is an exact duplicate of the old one.

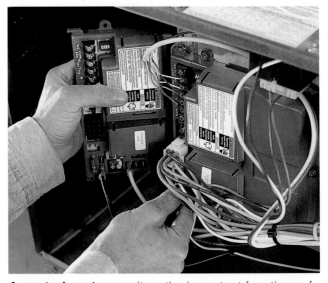

A control center monitors the important functions of a furnace. Call the furnace manufacturer if you suspect the control center needs to be replaced. To replace a control center, shut off power to the furnace at the main service panel. Detach the wires from the old control center one at a time, attach them to the replacement, and install the new unit.

Maintaining a Furnace Humidifier

Most furnace humidifiers are one of two types: *drum-style* and *drip-style*. A drum-style humidifier has a rotating drum that picks up water from a reservoir pan. Air in the heating system passes through the drum and carries away water vapor to moisturize the air. A float controls the water level in the reservoir. In a drip-style humidifier, fresh water flows into a distribution tray and trickles through an evaporator pad. Any moisture that's not carried away by the air drains into a drain tube.

Drum-style models generally require more maintenance, because the standing water in the reservoir needs to be changed to prevent mold and algae growth. But both types need regular inspections and cleaning. Check the drum or pad once a month and replace it at the end of the heating season.

Everything You Need:

Tools: Tape measure, open-end wrench, chisel, putty knife.

Materials: (as needed) Vinegar, replacement drum pad, replacement evaporator pad.

Humidifiers attach to the furnace's air supply or return duct and are controlled by a humidistat that detects moisture levels in the ambient air.

How to Maintain a Drum-Style Humidifier

1 Shut off power to the furnace at the main service panel, and turn off the water supply to the humidifier. Remove the humidifier cover. If your owner's manual recommends a specific water level for the reservoir pan, use a tape measure to check the depth. Otherwise, see that there's enough water to soak the bottom of the drum.

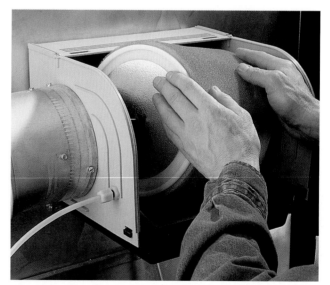

2 Inspect the drum pad. If it's stiff or dirty, clean or replace it. Carefully lift out the drum, using both hands.

(continued next page)

How to Maintain a Drum-style Humidifier (continued)

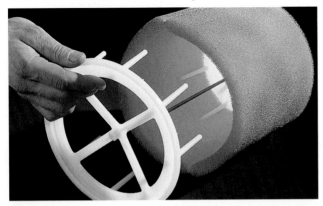

3 Remove the retaining clip or nut on the end of the drum shaft, and pull the drum ends from the shaft. Soak the pad in a 3:1 solution of vinegar and water, squeezing the pad to loosen deposits. Rinse the pad with clear water. If the pad is still stiff, replace it.

4 Remove the reservoir pan and clean it thoroughly. If you need to adjust the water level, loosen the screw on the float mount. Raise the float to increase the water level; lower the float to decrease it. Tighten the screw and replace the drum and cover.

How to Maintain a Drip-style Humidifier

1 Shut off power to the furnace at the main service panel, and turn off the water supply to the humidifier. Remove the humidifier cover, and disconnect the water supply tube from the distribution tray. Pull the distribution tray from the evaporator assembly.

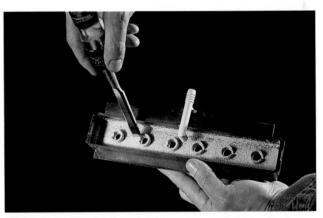

2 Use a chisel to remove any mineral deposits from the V-notches on the distribution tray.

3 Slide the evaporator pad out of its frame. Twist and flex the pad to loosen deposits. If necessary, use a putty knife to remove deposits. If the pad itself crumbles, replace it.

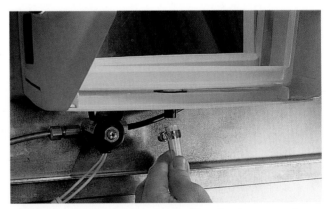

4 Disconnect the drain hose. Flex the hose, and flush it with cold water. Reattach the drain hose, and reassemble the humidifier.

Repairing Electric Baseboard Heaters

A baseboard heater (right), is a simple electrical unit consisting of a heating *element*, with attached metal *fins* for transferring heat, and a *limit control*–a switch that prevents the element from overheating. To control the temperature, some models have a built-in thermostat; others are controlled only by a *line voltage*, or *zone* thermostat (see page 54)—a wall mounted thermostat that is wired directly to the heater.

Most baseboard heaters and their thermostats are wired to a 240-volt circuit, which means both the black and white circuit wires are hot and carry voltage. Others use 120 volts, and are wired to a circuit or plugged into a standard receptacle. The tests for all three types are virtually the same.

If your baseboard heater is wired to a household circuit, shut off the power to the unit at the main service panel (page 33), then test for power before proceeding (right, below).

Note: Wiring for heater units and built-in thermostats may vary. For the best—and safest—results, check the manufacturer's wiring instructions, and label all wires before disconnecting them.

Everything You Need:

Tools: Screwdrivers, neon circuit tester, multi-tester, vacuum or brush, needlenose pliers.

Materials: (as needed) Replacement parts, masking tape, pen

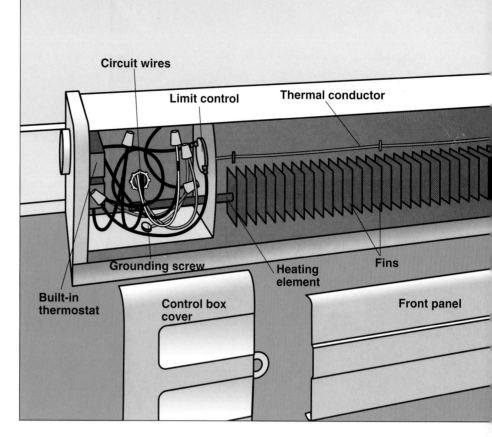

Circuit wires
Limit control
Thermal conductor
Grounding screw
Heating element
Fins
Built-in thermostat
Control box cover
Front panel

How to Test for Power Before Making Repairs

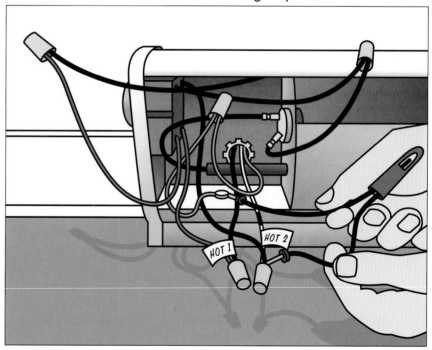

HOT 1   HOT 2

Turn off the power to the heater at the main service panel (page 33). Remove the heater's control box cover, and label the black hot circuit wire. Insert one probe of a neon circuit tester into the wire connector at the end of the circuit wire, and touch the other probe to the grounding screw on the heater casing. Then, label the other circuit wire (with a 240-volt heater, this wire will also carry voltage). Insert the tester probe into its wire connector, and touch the other probe to the grounding screw. Finally, insert one probe into each of the wire connectors you've just tested. If the tester glows for any of the tests, the power is still on. Return to the service panel and shut off the correct circuit.

115

How to Clean the Fins

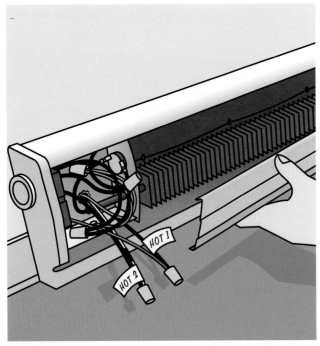

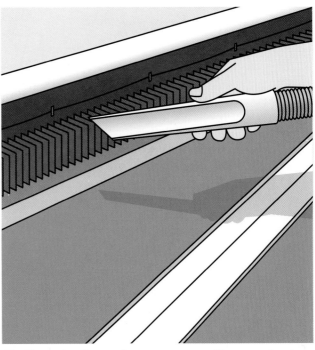

1 Clean and straighten the fins to improve the heater's efficiency and prevent overheating. First, shut off the power to the heater at the main service panel, then confirm that the power is off (page 115). Remove the front panel covering the heating element.

2 Clean the fins, using a vacuum with a nozzle attachment or a soft-bristle brush. Use needlenose pliers to straighten badly bent fins. Reattach the front cover and restore power to the heater.

How to Test & Replace the Limit Control

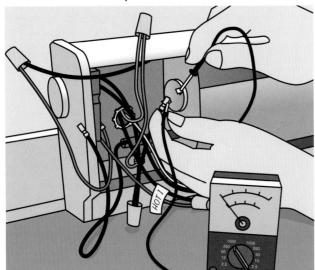

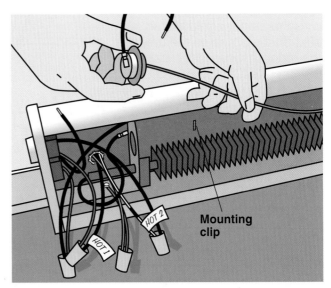

Mounting clip

1 Test the limit control if the heater doesn't turn on or seems to overheat. Shut off power at the main service panel, and confirm that the power is off (page 115). Disconnect one of the wires from its terminal on the limit control. Set a multi-tester to test for continuity, then touch one probe to each of the limit control terminals. The tester needle should move to ZERO, indicating continuity. If not, replace the limit control.

2 Remove the front panel covering the heating element. Disconnect the remaining wire from the limit control, and remove the screws or bend out the tabs securing the limit control to the unit. Pull the thermal conductor from each of its mounting clips, then slide the limit control from the unit. Replace the limit control with a duplicate part from the manufacturer.

How to Test a Built-in Thermostat

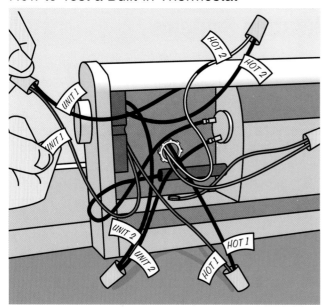

1 Test the thermostat if the heater won't respond when you adjust the knob and you're sure the limit control works. Shut off power at the main service panel, and confirm the power is off (page 115). Label each thermostat lead and the wire connected to it, giving both wires the same name. Designate the circuit wires and their respective leads as "HOT," and the heater wires and their respective leads as "UNIT." Disconnect the wires and remove the thermostat.

2 Set a multi-tester to test for continuity, then turn the thermostat dial to the highest (hottest) setting. Touch one tester probe to a "HOT" wire lead, and touch the other probe to each of the "UNIT" wires. During one of the connections, the tester needle should move to ZERO, indicating continuity. Next, touch one probe to the other "HOT" wire lead, and the other probe to each of the "UNIT" wires. Again, there should be continuity with one of the connections. If the thermostat fails either test, replace it with a duplicate part from the manufacturer.

How to Test the Heating Element

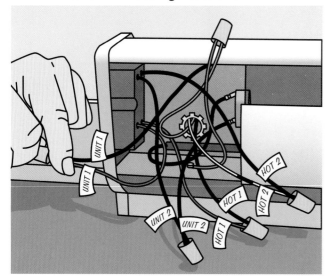

1 If the limit control and thermostat are working, but there's still no heat, test the heating element. Shut off the power at the main service panel, and confirm that the power is off (page 115). Find the heating element wire that is connected to one of the thermostat leads. (This wire may be coming from the far end of the heating element.) Unscrew the wire connector and separate the wires.

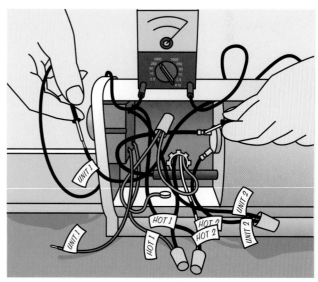

2 Set a multi-tester to test for continuity. Touch one tester probe to the free heating element wire, and touch the other probe to the wire running from the limit control to the other end of the element. The tester needle should move to ZERO, indicating continuity. If so, the heating element is sound, and the problem may lie in the circuit. If not, the element is bad, and you should replace the entire unit.

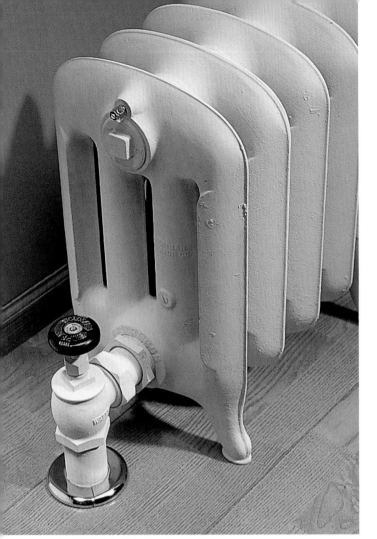

Maintaining Hot Water Heating Systems

Hot water heating systems use a boiler that heats water and circulates it through a system of pipes to the radiators or convectors around the house. These systems are low-maintenance, but there are a few important tasks that keep your system running efficiently. In the event of leaky pipes or boiler problems, call a professional.

Trapped air accumulates in a hot water system and must be released to maintain efficiency. This technique, known as "bleeding," can also quiet noisy radiators. Bleed all the radiators in your house once a year, and bleed an individual unit if it stays cold when the heat is on. Some convector units have similar bleed valves.

Rust and sediment can accumulate in a heating system, inhibiting the water's flow and reducing efficiency. To extend the life of the system, drain and fill the boiler once a year. This requires shutting down the system for a while, and it can be a smelly job, so it's best to drain a boiler during the summer when you can keep the windows open.

Hot-water radiators have a supply pipe with a shut-off valve usually connected near the bottom of the unit. Bleed the radiators each fall to release trapped air (below, right).

Everything You Need:

Tools: Screwdriver or valve key, wrenches, funnel.

Materials: Towel, rust inhibitor, elbow fitting.

How to Service Convectors

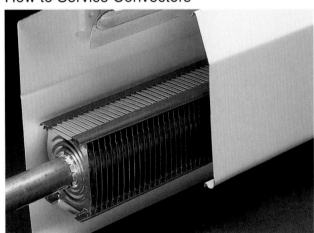

Hot-water convectors are water pipes with thin metal fins attached for radiating heat. Clean dust and debris from convector fins regularly to ensure maximum efficiency. Individual convectors may have bleed valves for releasing trapped air in the system. If not, ask a plumber about having the system bled.

How to Bleed Hot-water Radiators

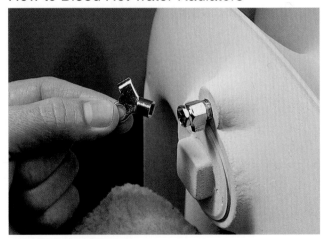

Turn up the thermostat so the heating systems runs. Start at the radiator that's the highest in the house and farthest from the boiler. Hold a towel under the bleed valve, and open the valve using the knob (if provided), a screwdriver, or a valve key (available at hardware stores). When water squirts out, close the valve. Bleed the next farthest radiator, and so on, until all radiators are bled.

How to Drain & Fill a Hot-Water Boiler

1 Shut off power to the boiler at the main service panel (page 33). If the system is hot, let it cool for a few hours. Shut off the water supply to the boiler. Attach one end of a garden hose to the drain at the bottom of the boiler; place the other end in a floor drain or utility sink. Open the boiler drain valve, then open the bleed valve on the highest radiator in the house (page 118). When water stops draining from the boiler, open the bleed valve on a radiator closer to the boiler.

2 When the water flow stops again, locate the gauge or valve near the top of the boiler. Remove the gauge or valve—you may need one or two wrenches for the job.

3 Purchase a rust inhibitor from a heating supply dealer, and read the instructions on the container. Close the boiler drain valve. Using a funnel—and a temporary elbow fitting, if necessary—add the recommended amount of rust inhibitor through the gauge or valve fitting. Reinstall the gauge or valve, and close all radiator bleed valves.

4 Slowly open the water supply to the boiler. When the water pressure gauge reads 5 psi, bleed the radiators on the first floor, then bleed those on the upper floors. Allow the boiler pressure to reach 20 psi, then turn on the power. Adjust the thermostat to run the heating system. After the system completes several cycles, bleed the radiators again.

Inspect the flue for large obstructions, such as animals and bird's nests. Open the damper, and use a mirror and a shop light to get a good view. Also look with the shop light off: you should be able to see light coming in from the top of the flue. If you find any blockage, have the flue professionally cleaned before using the fireplace.

Cleaning & Inspecting Fireplaces

The most important cleaning and inspection of your fireplace and chimney should be done by a certified chimney sweep. A good service will check the firebox, damper, flue, and stack—the exterior structure around the flue—in addition to giving the flue a thorough brush-cleaning. Have this done every one to two years, depending on how much you use the fireplace. Schedule the service before winter, so snow and ice don't prevent the sweep from getting on the roof.

If it's been a while since you've used your fireplace, conduct your own inspection of the damper and flue before starting a fire. Make sure the flue is unobstructed and the damper opens all the way and makes a complete seal when it's closed.

Everything You Need:

Tools: Mirror, shop light, flashlight, stiff brush, shovel, spray bottle.

Materials: Non-porous container.

Check the damper for full operation. Open the damper all the way to check for obstructions, then close it, and use a flashlight (or a shop light and mirror) to make sure the opening is tightly sealed. A closed damper prevents the escape of warm room air when the fireplace is not in use. If necessary, scrub around the damper plate and opening with a stiff brush to remove any buildup that is preventing a tight seal.

Empty the ash pit once a year. Ash pit cleanout doors are usually located in the basement or on an exterior wall. Scoop the ashes into a non-porous container, and use a spray bottle of water to keep the dust down.

Maintaining & Repairing Ventilation Systems

Ventilation devices in your home do more than provide a comfortable atmosphere. Exhaust fans carry away excess moisture, harmful gasses, and airborne dust and germs. Ceiling fans circulate air in individual rooms and keep heated or cooled air where you want it. *Air exchangers* (below right) are increasingly popular devices that circulate fresh air through a home's ductwork.

During mild weather, open windows provide good ventilation, but when a house is sealed, trapped air quickly goes stale, especially in newer homes. That's why it's important to maintain—and use—your home's ventilation devices. Most require little maintenance other than routine cleaning and filter replacement. Turn to page 122 for advice on tuning up a ceiling fan.

Everything You Need:

Tools: Screwdriver, wrench, tape measure.

Materials: (as needed) Ceiling fan balancing kit.

Watch for signs of poor ventilation. Sweaty windows during the heating season are an indication of trapped moisture. In bathrooms, kitchens, and laundry rooms, look for condensation in the winter and mildew in the summer; these can usually be corrected by installing an exhaust fan or vent hose.

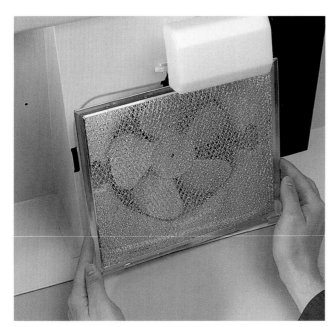

Clean exhaust filters and fans regularly to ensure maximum ventilation. Remove filters and grills from fan units and soak them in hot, soapy water to remove grease and dust. Wipe fan blades thoroughly: a clean fan is more balanced, runs quieter, and moves air more effectively than a dirty one.

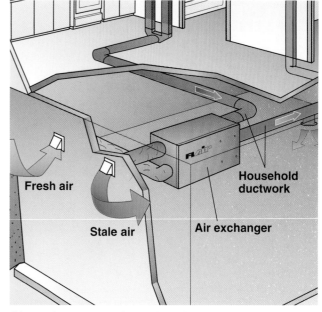

Fresh air

Stale air

Household ductwork

Air exchanger

Air exchangers—also called *heat-recovery ventilators*—borrow heat from stale indoor air as it exits the house and use it to warm incoming fresh air. Air exchangers also filter the fresh air as it enters the system. If you have an air exchanger, check the filter once a month during the heating season. Be sure to shut off the power to the exchanger before opening the filter cover.

How to Repair a Ceiling Fan

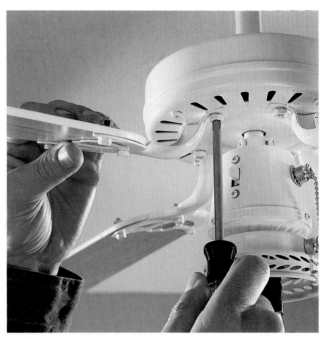

Ceiling fans wobble when the blades are loose, off-set, or unbalanced. Tighten and adjust the blades, then balance them, if necessary, to quiet the fan and improve its operation. If the glass globe rattles, take it down and fit a thick rubber band over the neck of the globe. Reinstall the globe, making sure the mounting screws are even and tight.

1 Tighten the screws holding the blade connecting brackets to the motor unit, and tighten the bolts securing the blades to the brackets. Test the fan. If it still wobbles, proceed to step 2.

2 Measure the blades to make sure they're level. Hold a tape measure to the ceiling, and measure the distance between the ceiling and the end of a blade. Keeping the tape measure in the same spot, rotate the fan and check the remaining blades. To make a correction, gently bend the blade brackets until all blades are the same distance from the ceiling. If the fan still wobbles, go to step 3.

3 Buy a blade balancing kit from a hardware store or home center. Attach the clip from the kit to the middle of the rear edge of a blade. Turn on the fan and note whether the wobble increases or decreases. Use the clip to test all of the blades, adjusting the clip's position to find the locations where it helps the most. Attach a weight from the kit to the top side of the blades at each of these locations.

122

Maintaining & Repairing Air Conditioning Systems

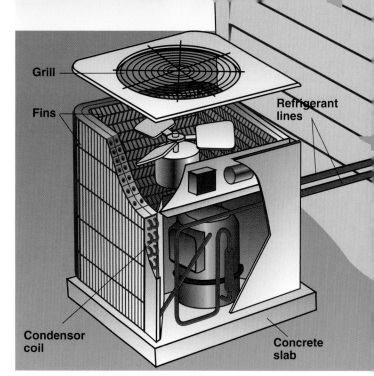

Central air conditioners and heat pumps are similar, and routine maintenance for either is virtually the same. The systems differ in that heat pumps can also heat the house during cold weather. What makes this possible is the *reversing valve*, which you can check and, if necessary, replace, should your heat pump supply heat in the summer or cool air in the winter. Room air conditioners aren't exposed to as many harmful elements as central units, but a quick monthly inspection and filter cleaning will increase their cooling power and longevity.

Check your air conditioning unit or heat pump regularly, depending on how much you use it. If you cool the air several months a year or use a heat pump for both heating and cooling, check the outdoor unit monthly. Otherwise, give it a thorough cleaning and inspection each spring. Always check the air filter in your home's ductwork or furnace, as well. For other important maintenance tasks, such as checking refrigerant levels, call a professional.

Caution: Air conditioning units (including room models) and heat pumps contain one or more *capacitors*–devices that store electricity. After shutting off the power, **wait at least 5 minutes** for the capacitor to discharge its stored electricity before you work on the unit.

Air conditioners circulate a refrigerant between an *evaporator* (indoors) and a *condenser* (outdoors). Blown by the furnace or other circulator, air is cooled as it passes through the evaporator on its way to the home's air duct system. Heat is transferred from the refrigerant *coils* through thin metal *fins*.

Everything You Need:

Tools: Screwdrivers, nut drivers, soft brush, fin comb, open-end wrenches, level, vacuum, multi-tester.

Materials: (as needed) Cloth, all-purpose household oil, gloves, replacement parts.

How to Maintain a Central Air Conditioning or Heat Pump Unit

1 Shut off the unit's power switch, found on an exterior wall near the unit. Also turn off power to the air conditioning system at the main service panel (page 33). Wait 5 minutes for the capacitor to discharge.

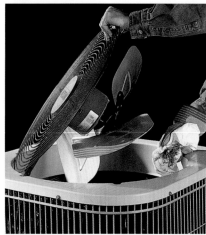

2 Remove the screws securing the top grill, and lift up the grill. Clean dirt and debris from inside the unit as well as from the fan and motor. Remove the side grill that surrounds the unit. Use a cloth and soft brush to remove dirt and debris from the fins and coil.

3 Use a fin comb to straighten any bent or flattened fins. Hold the comb near the fins to select the correct comb size and spacing.

(continued next page)

4 Lubricate the fan motor. If the motor is attached to the grill, the ports will be located above the fan blades. Remove the plugs covering the oil ports, and add three drops of all-purpose oil to each port. Reinstall the plugs.

5 Wearing gloves, spin the fan to check for smooth rotation. If the fan is loose, tighten the setscrew on the motor shaft. If the fan is bent, remove it from the shaft and replace it with an exact duplicate.

6 Check the concrete slab supporting the unit. The slab should lean slightly away from the house, to facilitate drainage. When the slab is set properly, check the top of the unit to make sure it is level. To level the unit, use the unit's adjustable feet, if it has them, or install shims under the feet.

How to Check & Replace a Heat Pump Reversing Valve Solenoid

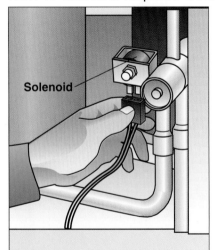

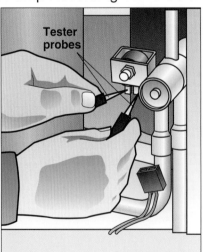

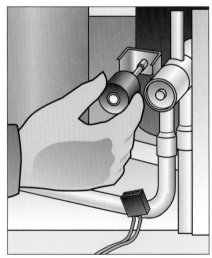

1 Shut off the unit's power switch (page 123) and turn off the power at the main service panel. Wait 5 minutes. Remove the access panel at the back of the unit. Disconnect the plug attached to the solenoid contacts.

2 Set a multi-tester (page 56) to to test for continuity. Place a tester probe on each of the solenoid contacts. The tester needle should move to ZERO, indicating continuity. If not, the solenoid is faulty.

3 To replace the solenoid, remove the retaining nut on the solenoid housing, and remove the solenoid. Purchase a duplicate part from the manufacturer. Install the new solenoid, and reattach the plug and access panel.

How to Maintain a Room Air Conditioner

1 Unplug the unit and let it sit for at least 5 minutes. Then, remove the front cover containing the air filter. Carefully remove the filter from the cover.

2 Check the filter label for washing instructions; most can be vacuumed or washed in water and mild detergent. Dry the filter by blotting it with a clean cloth, and reinstall it when it has dried completely.

3 Remove the panel from the back of the unit to expose the condenser fins. You may have to pull the unit from the wall or window to access the back panel. Clean the fins with a vacuum and soft brush attachment. Straighten any bent fins with a fin comb.

4 Clean the drain pan with a cloth. Check the drain hole or hose and clear any blockage. Reattach the back panel.

Exterior Home Repairs

Making Exterior Home Repairs

Regardless of where you live, the greatest threat to your home's exterior is water. In any form—rain, ice, or snow—water eventually damages everything it touches. And because water never stops, neither do the maintenance chores required to protect your home from the damage it causes. The best way to minimize damage is to direct water off all surfaces and away from the house.

To assess how well your house manages water, visualize the path rain water takes, starting at the peak of the roof and flowing downward. Do the shingles and flashing create an impervious skin for shedding water? Are the gutters clean and straight? Is the siding well painted and the trim sealed with caulk at the joints?

Most importantly, look for signs of damage. Rotted, split, or cracked wood, chipped paint, and holes or cracks in concrete and masonry allow water deeper into the material, compounding damage over time. Repair problem areas, and look for ways to minimize water's access to them in the future. Small steps could save a great deal of time and money in the long run.

Touch up areas where paint has failed or worn away. Remove old peeling or chipped paint with a scraper or stiff brush, and apply a primer to any bare wood before painting. For many exterior wood features, paint is the only defense against the elements.

Apply caulk wherever water can get in. Seal around door and window frames, cover joints between siding and trim boards, and fill gaps around intervening elements, such as pipes and vents.

Patch damaged surfaces with exterior-rated patching compound. Deep cracks and gouges absorb a lot of water. If wood is rotted, cut out or replace the rotted material, and apply a paintable wood preservative before painting.

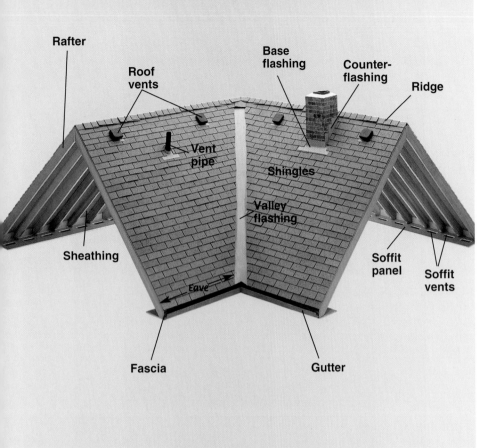

Rafter
Roof vents
Base flashing
Counter-flashing
Ridge
Vent pipe
Shingles
Valley flashing
Sheathing
Eave
Soffit panel
Soffit vents
Fascia
Gutter

Repairing Roofs

The elements of a roof system work together to provide shelter, drainage, and ventilation. The roof covering is composed of wood planks or plywood sheathing, building paper, and shingles. Metal flashing, attached in valleys and around intervening elements, slips under the shingles to seal out water. Fascia boards cover the rafter ends and receive the soffit panels, which enclose the undersides of the eaves.

How to Make an Emergency Roof Repair

Use plastic sheeting or a tarp to create an emergency roof patch. Slip the top edge of plastic under a row of shingles, then secure all of the edges with nailed strips of wood. Be sure to patch the nail holes with roofing cement after you remove the nails.

Of all the elements of your house, the roof endures the most exposure to the elements, yet it's easy to forget that a roof needs regular maintenance. Thanks to water and gravity, however, roof problems don't go unnoticed for long.

Stopping and preventing leaks are priorities in roof maintenance, of course, but it's important to remember that roofs are responsible for more than shelter—they also ventilate most of the warm, moist air that rises from the home's interior. Roof systems use vents—usually found along soffit panels and up near the ridge—to keep down humidity levels and maintain a temperature balance between the attic and the outdoors.

Common signs of poor ventilation include ice dams, condensation or mildew on the roof's underside, and an attic that stays hot in cold weather. If you discover any of these symptoms, call a building professional who specializes in home environment and weatherization issues. Every house is different, and problems may involve more than ventilation.

Everything You Need:

Tools: Awl, hammer, pry bar, chisel, hacksaw blade, paintbrush.

Materials: Wood block, bucket, roofing cement, 1" and 1¼" galvanized roofing nails, mineral spirits, baking soda.

Tips for Locating & Minimizing Water Damage

To locate the source of a leak, inspect the roof rafters for water tracks and discoloration. Make a mark at the highest point where water penetration is evident (see below, right).

If water is flowing down the side of a rafter, nail a block of wood to divert the water's path. Place a bucket underneath to catch the water. Check the bucket frequently to make sure it doesn't overflow.

If water is dripping onto a finished ceiling surface, punch a hole with an awl or a nail to release the water into a bucket.

On a dry day, locate problem areas by driving nails through the underside of the sheathing or by transferring measurements taken from inside the house. Measure from common elements, such as the roof peak or intervening pipes. Seal all nail holes with roofing cement.

Tips for Making Spot Repairs with Roofing Cement

Use roofing cement—a tar-like compound—for a variety of minor repairs. To reattach a loose shingle, wipe off any dirt and minerals from the building paper and underside of the shingle. Make sure the surfaces are dry, then liberally apply roofing cement. Press the shingle into the bed of cement.

Tack down buckled shingles by cleaning out below the buckled area, filling with roofing cement, and pressing the shingle into the cement. Also use roofing cement to patch cracks or other minor shingle problems.

Seal gaps around flashing by cleaning out the old roofing cement and replacing it with fresh cement. Joints around flashing are common causes of leaks.

Run a bead of roofing cement along edges where shingles meet flashing. Seal the edges at the valley flashing and along the *drip edge*—the flashing underneath the first row of shingles (along the eave).

How to Replace Asphalt Shingles

1 Pull out the damaged shingles in the repair area, beginning with the uppermost shingle. Be careful not to damage any surrounding shingles that are in good condition.

2 Remove old nails with a flat pry bar (exposed nail heads could puncture the new shingles). Remove nails in the shingle above the repair area to enable you to install new shingles. Cover holes or repair damage in the building paper with roofing cement.

3 Install the replacement shingles, beginning with the lowest one. Nail above the tab slots with 1" galvanized roofing nails.
Tip: Before installing asphalt shingles, "age" them to match the surrounding area. Rub shingles with mineral spirits, then rinse them.

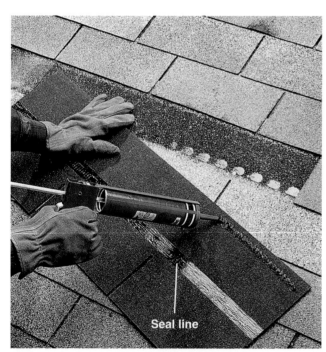

Seal line

4 Install all but the top replacement shingle with nails, then apply roofing cement to the underside of the top replacement shingle, above the seal line.

5 Slip the top shingle into place, and press down to create a good bond with the roofing cement. Lift up the overlapping shingle above, and nail the top replacement shingle in place. Also, renail the shingles above the repair area, then patch any remaining nail holes with roofing cement.

How to Replace Wood Shakes & Shingles

1 Split apart the damaged shakes or shingles with a chisel and hammer, and pull out the loose pieces. Slide a hacksaw blade underneath the shingle above, and cut off the nails flush with the lower shingle surface.

2 If you're replacing more than one row of shingles, you can nail the first replacement row with 1¼" galvanized roofing nails. Be sure to stagger the joints between shingle rows, so that each shingle overlaps a joint below.

3 Use roofing cement to secure the final row of shingles. Apply cement to both sides of the shingles, covering the area that will be overlapped by the shingles above. Slide the shingles into place, then press down to bond the cement.

Tip: To "age" new shakes and shingles so they blend in with the rest of the roof, mix a pound of baking soda in a gallon of water. Brush the solution onto the shingles, then place them in direct sunlight for four or five hours. Rinse them thoroughly and let them dry.

Fixing Gutters & Solving Drainage Problems

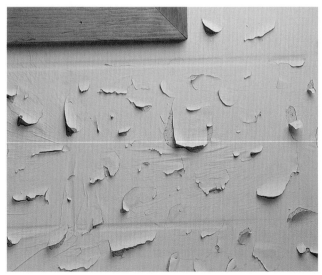

Stains on exterior walls indicate that a gutter is leaking or overflowing due to blockage. Regularly cleaning and maintaining the gutters helps protect your house, from the roof to the basement.

Everything You Need:

Tools: Trowel, level, chalk line, pry bar, drill, hammer, wire brush, putty knife, hacksaw, shovel, rake.

Materials: Hose, roofing cement, abrasive pad, downspout section, 2 × 4, soil.

Gutter systems play a critical role in protecting both the exterior and interior of your house. By catching runoff water from the roof, gutters keep the siding dry. They also prevent water from pooling around the foundation—the most common cause of wet basements.

For gutters to work properly, they need to be clean and sound, and they should slope toward the downspouts to ensure water flow. Downspouts must extend well beyond the house to distribute water away from the foundation.

The ground around the foundation also has a role in protecting your house—it must slope downward to direct water away from the foundation. If your basement floods during storms or you find moisture on your foundation's walls, check the grade around the foundation, and make sure any walkways and other surfaces slope away from the house.

Peeling paint on basement walls is a sign that moisture is trapped behind the paint. This is usually caused by water that has pooled around the foundation and is seeping through the wall.

Puddles on walkways occur when concrete slabs settle and prevent water runoff. Standing water damages concrete and adjoining materials and may contribute to foundation flooding.

133

How to Clean & Inspect Gutters & Downspouts

1 Clean leaves, twigs and other material out of rain gutters, using a trowel. Debris in gutters can hold moisture and cause galvanized metal gutters to rust.

2 Flush out debris by inserting a garden hose into the downspout and turning on the water. Check for rust in the gutter, and patch any holes (page 135).

3 Check the slope of the gutters with a level. Gutters should angle toward the downspouts at a rate of $\frac{1}{16}$" per foot, or 1" in 16'.

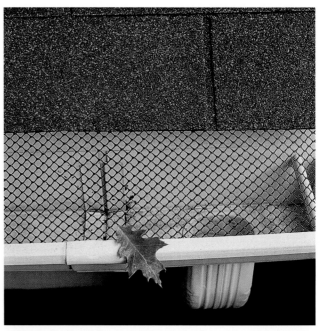

4 Shield gutters to keep out leaves and other debris and minimize cleanup. There are a number of gutter-shield systems available for all different types of gutters.

How to Lift Sagging Gutters

Snap a chalk line onto the fascia, following the proper slope for the gutter. Remove the hangers around the sagging area, and lift the gutter until it's flush with the chalk line. Reattach the hangers, using new holes. Add hangers, if necessary, so there is one hanger every 24" and within 12" of every seam.

To remove spike-type hangers, place a wood spacer into the gutter near the hanger. Use a pry bar padded by a wood shim to pull out the spike. Drill new pilot holes for the spikes, and fill the old holes with roofing cement.

How to Patch Metal Gutters

1 Clean the area around the damage with a wire brush. Scrub with an abrasive pad to loosen any residue, then clean the area with water and let it dry.

2 Apply a ⅛"-thick layer of roofing cement evenly over the damage, then spread it a few inches beyond the damaged area on all sides.

3 Cut and bend a patch from flashing made out of the same material as the gutter. Bed the patch in the cement, and feather the cement so it won't cause significant damming.

How to Extend Downspouts

Extend short downspouts, which otherwise deposit water right next to the foundation. Add an extension to downspouts to direct runoff water away from the foundation. Install an elbow on the end of the downspout, if it doesn't already have one.

2 Use a hacksaw to cut a 6'- to 8'-long section of downspout. A hacksaw will cut through either galvanized metal or plastic downspouts.

3 Fit one end of the new section over the downspout elbow. Secure the extension with two short, self-tapping sheet metal screws—one on each side.

4 Rest the free end of the extension on a splash block to disperse the water onto the lawn.

How to Check & Correct a Foundation Grade

1 Tape a level to a straight, 8'-long 2 × 4, and use it to check the grade around the entire house. The grade should slope away from the foundation (see step 3); if it is level, water can seep into the basement or crawlspace.

2 If necessary, add soil around the foundation to increase the slope away from the foundation. Rake the soil smooth, and recheck the grade.

Downspout extension

3 For a proper slope, the outside end of the 2 × 4 should be at least 6" above the ground when the board is level. In areas that are difficult to grade, add a downspout extension to help with water drainage (page 136).

Check the slope of concrete walkways, stoops, or patios. If the slab is level or slopes toward the foundation, consider having it raised, or *mud-jacked,* by a concrete contractor.

Specialty tools for concrete and masonry repairs include: masonry chisels (1), masonry hammers (2), concrete floats (3), concrete finishing tools (4), jointing tool (5), drill with masonry bits, grinding disc, and masonry-cutting blade (6), and masonry trowels (7).

Everything You Need:

Tools: Drill, masonry-grinding disc, paintbrush, hammer, masonry chisel, trowels, circular saw, masonry-cutting blade, wood float, concrete edger, mortar raking tool, mortar hawk, joint filler, jointing tool, stiff nylon brush, wire brush, wisk broom.

Materials: Paint thinner, concrete caulk, anchoring cement, latex bonding agent, vinyl-reinforced patching compound, sand, sand-mix concrete, concrete fortifier, plywood, vegetable oil, quick-setting cement, Type N mortar, metal primer, stucco repair compound.

Tip for Cleaning Concrete

Clean up oil stains by dampening sawdust with paint thinner, then spreading the sawdust over the stain. The thinner will dissolve the oil, allowing it to be absorbed by the sawdust.

Repairing Concrete & Masonry

Concrete, brick, and stucco—the three stalwarts of home construction—are exceptionally durable. Like most materials, they do have natural enemies, most notably, water, seasonal freeze-thaw cycles, and the shifting of the soil or underlying structure.

As a highly rigid material, concrete is susceptible to cracking. Cracks let water inside, where it erodes the material or freezes and expands, enlarging the crack with each cycle. But concrete repairs are relatively easy, and with the right products, most repairs are permanent.

Aside from structural problems caused by settling, brick structures and surfaces suffer most from deterioration of mortar joints. In fact, mortar is designed to weather and wear faster than brick. *Tuckpointing,* a technique for restoring failed mortar joints, is an effective way to maintain walls, chimneys, brick veneer, or any other structure where brick or block is bonded with mortar.

Stucco is somewhat like plaster for exterior walls, and as with plaster, major repairs are best left to professionals. But filling cracks and patching small holes in stucco walls can help you avoid expensive repairs in the future.

Tips for Repairing Concrete

Use concrete repair caulk for quick repairs to minor cracks (up to ¼"-wide). Repair caulk seals out water to prevent further damage, but should be used only for temporary repairs. On horizontal surfaces, use a liquid concrete seal, which dries to look like concrete. Turn to page 140 for help with larger cracks.

Reset loose anchors with anchoring cement. Remove the anchors, and fill the old holes with the cement, which expands as it dries. Press the anchors into the wet cement and let it set completely.

How to Patch Holes in Concrete

1 Cut out around the damaged area with a masonry-grinding disc and a drill, or use a hammer and masonry chisel. Undercut the hole by beveling the cuts about 15° away from the center of the hole. Chisel out any loose material and sweep sand and dirt from the hole.

2 Use a paintbrush to coat the repair area with latex bonding agent. Then, use a trowel to fill the hole with vinyl-reinforced concrete patching compound, applied in layers no thicker than ½". Wait 30 minutes between layers, and slightly overfill the hole. Feather out the patch so it's flush with the surrounding surface.

How to Fill Cracks in Concrete

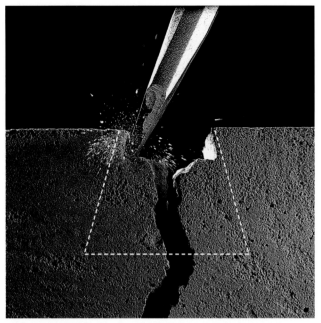

1 Use a patching compound for cracks over ¼" wide. First, undercut the sides of the crack, using a masonry chisel and hammer or a circular saw and masonry-cutting blade. The angled cut helps to lock in the repair patch. Remove any loose material, and brush out any sand or dirt from the crack.

2 Apply latex bonding agent to the crack, using a paintbrush. Mix vinyl-reinforced patching compound, following the manufacturer's instructions, then trowel the compound into the crack, overfilling it slightly. Feather the compound so the patch is flush with the surrounding surface.

Tips for Repairing Larger Cracks

To patch deep cracks, prepare the crack (step 1, above), then fill the crack with sand to within ½" of the surface. Coat the area with latex bonding agent. Combine sand-mix concrete with a concrete fortifier additive, which provides flexibility to resist cracking. Trowel the patching mixture into the crack, and feather it flush with the surface.

Patch wide cracks (over ¼") on vertical surfaces using vinyl patching compound. Prepare the crack (step 1, above), then use a paintbrush to apply a layer of latex bonding agent. Mix a batch of compound, following the manufacturer's directions, then press the compound deep into the crack with a narrow tool, slightly overfilling it. Feather the patch flush with the surface, using a trowel.

How to Patch Concrete Steps

1 Make a cut in the step tread just outside the damaged area, using a circular saw with a masonry-cutting blade. Angle the cut toward the back of the step to undercut the edge. Make a similar cut on the riser below the damaged area, then chisel out the area in between the two cuts.

2 Cut a plywood form board the same height as the step riser, then coat one side of the board with vegetable oil to prevent the patch from sticking. Set the board against the riser of the damaged step, and brace it in position with heavy blocks. Make sure the top of the form is flush with the top of the step tread.

3 Mix quick-setting cement following the manufacturer's instructions, and be sure to check the setting and drying times for the product. Use a wet sponge to dampen the repair area. Press the wet cement into the area with a trowel, packing it firmly.

4 Smooth off the cement with a concrete float, and let it set until it's firm enough to retain a thumbprint. Round over the front edge of the nose with an edger, and use a trowel to smooth the sides of the patch. Remove the form board, and smooth the patch so it's flush with the riser. Allow the cement to cure completely before using the step.

How to Tuckpoint Mortar Joints

1 Clean out loose or deteriorated mortar to a depth of ¼" to ¾". Use a mortar raking tool (top) first, then switch to a masonry chisel and a hammer (bottom) if the mortar is stubborn. Clear away all loose material, and dampen the surface with water before applying fresh Type N mortar.

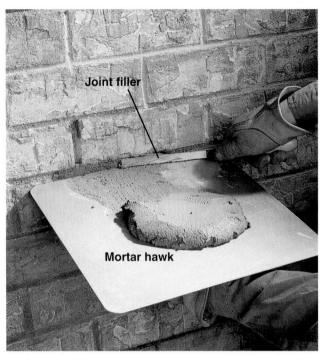

Joint filler

Mortar hawk

2 Mix the mortar, adding concrete fortifier. If necessary, add tint to match original mortar. Load mortar onto a mortar hawk or piece of wood, then push it into the horizontal joints, using a joint filler. Apply mortar in ¼"-thick layers, and let each layer dry for 30 minutes before applying another. Fill the joints until the mortar is flush with the face of the brick or block.

3 Apply the first layer of mortar into the vertical joints by scooping mortar onto the back of the joint filler, and pressing it into the joint. Work from the top of the repair area downward.

4 After applying the final layer of mortar, smooth the joints with a jointing tool that matches the profile of the old joints. Tool the horizontal joints first, then the vertical. Let the mortar dry until it is crumbly, then brush off the excess mortar with a stiff nylon brush.

How to Repair Stucco

Fill thin cracks with concrete caulk, which stays semi-flexible and prevents further cracking. Overfill the crack slightly, and feather the caulk so it's flush with the surface. After it sets, paint the caulk to match the surrounding area.

1 To patch moderate damage, clean out loose material from the repair area with a wire brush. Remove rust from any exposed metal lath, and treat the lath with metal primer.

2 Trowel premixed stucco repair compound into the hole, using a putty knife or pointed trowel, and overfilling it slightly (read the manufacturer's directions—drying times and application may vary).

3 Smooth the patch with a putty knife or trowel, feathering it flush with the surrounding surface. Use a whisk broom or trowel to create a matching texture on the patch. After the patch dries, touch up the area with masonry paint.

Restoring Asphalt Surfaces

Asphalt driveways and walks become damaged by impact, water penetration, and seasonal freeze-thaw cycles. Water running under blacktop from the side or through cracks undermines the gravel base that supports the slab.

To repair asphalt and prevent further damage, fill holes and cracks with asphalt patcher, apply sealer to the surface, and fill washouts along the slab edge to keep the water out.

Everything You Need:

Tools: Vacuum, garden hose, heat gun, trowel, stiff brush, putty knife, squeegee/broom.

Materials: Asphalt cleaner, asphalt patcher, asphalt sealer.

How to Patch Holes in Asphalt

1 Remove dirt and debris from the hole with a shop vacuum. Flush out the hole with a garden hose and spray nozzle.

2 Pour asphalt patching material into the hole. Warm the material with a heat gun, then level and smooth the patch with a trowel.

3 Tamp the patch so it's packed firmly into the hole. Firm, smooth patches prevent future water damage.

How to Seal an Asphalt Drive

1 Fill any holes in the slab (page 144). Clean the slab with an asphalt cleaner to remove oil and dirt from surface. Rinse the surface with a hose or power washer.

2 Patch cracks in the asphalt using a caulk gun and a tube of asphalt patcher. Large cracks may need several applications.

3 Spread and smooth the patch material, using a putty knife. Dip the knife in cold water or mineral spirits to prevent the patcher from sticking to it.

4 Pour a puddle of asphalt sealer onto the slab and spread it, following the manufacturer's directions. A layer that's too thick will not cure properly; it's better to apply two coats.

5 Allow the sealer to cure fully before driving or walking on the slab. Block the drive with sawhorses or rope and ladders to prevent traffic during the drying period.

Home Security

Improving Home Security

Criminals are a fact of life. They're as much a part of our world as water and air. And, like these natural elements, criminals tend to follow the path of least resistance. This means that if a burglar is working his way down your street, and he finds your neighbor's house to be well secured—with outdoor lighting, highly visible points of entry, and adequate locks on the doors and windows—he'll pass it up and move on to your house. Does your home provide enough resistance to discourage a burglar?

Improving the security of your home starts with a simple inspection. Most homes have at least one vulnerable point of entry: a glass-paned door; a basement window hidden behind a wall of shrubs; an attached garage with an entry door that has no deadbolt. These are common examples of easy targets that invite burglars. Take a walk in and around your home, during the day and after dark, and look for easy targets. Think about how *you* would get in if you didn't have keys.

Inside the house, check all the doors and windows. Most break-ins occur through doors, so give them special attention. Outside, examine the house and grounds from the street, and the alley, if there is one. Are there places to hide? Are any doors or windows fully obscured from your view? Which windows are accessible from the ground? Could an agile person get up on the roof? How secure is the garage?

Most security problems are easy to solve. With a few lock installations or upgrades, some strategic lighting, and more thoughtful landscaping, you can dramatically increase your home's security—at little cost.

Option: Installing a Security Alarm

At some time or another, most homeowners are tempted to install a security alarm system. There is some evidence that alarm systems are an effective way to deter intruders. Professionally installed systems that automatically contact emergency operators can save valuable time in dispatching emergency vehicles to your home. But alarm systems can be expensive to install and maintain, and the more inexpensive models are prone to sending false alarms, which can result in substantial fines in some municipalities. If you are considering installing a security alarm system, first discuss your situation with a community officer from your local law enforcement agency.

Options for security alarm systems include:

Professionally installed alarm systems: Professional technicians will visit your home and work with you to decide what type of system best fits your needs. They will install and maintain the equipment. Most professionally installed systems will automatically contact the appropriate emergency department if the alarm is tripped. Initial installation costs vary, but can be fairly expensive. Monthly service fees usually are charged as well.

Owner-installed systems: Many manufacturers sell security alarm systems designed to be installed and maintained by homeowners. They vary from one or two simple sensors linked to a loud alarm horn, to fairly complex systems of sensors, alarms, and radio transmitters that often are wired into your home's electrical system. Consult with a security professional and shop to compare features and prices.

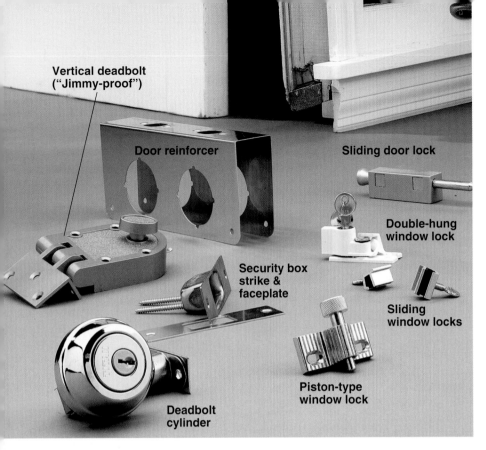

Vertical deadbolt ("Jimmy-proof")

Door reinforcer

Sliding door lock

Double-hung window lock

Security box strike & faceplate

Sliding window locks

Piston-type window lock

Deadbolt cylinder

Securing Doors & Windows

Securing doors and windows is simply a matter of having the right hardware. There are four basic elements in door security: the door, the lock, the frame, and the hinges. Skimping on strength or quality with any one of these will undermine the security of the whole system.

Entry doors should be metal or solid wood—at least 1¾" thick—and each one in the house should have a deadbolt lock, as doorknob locks provide little security. Lock quality covers a broad range; just make sure to choose one that has a bolt (or bolt core) of hardened steel and a minimum 1" *throw*—the distance the bolt protrudes from the door when engaged.

A lock is only as good as its mounting hardware: use long, sturdy screws for mounting locks to doors. Another important piece of hardware is the *strike plate*—the flat metal plate that receives the lock bolt. Standard strike plates are screwed into the door frame alone and may be backed by less than ½" of wood. For more strength, install a *security box strike.* This device has a deep metal pocket for supporting the bolt and includes long mounting screws that reach well into the wall studs.

Door hinges are easy to secure. You can add

plenty of strength by replacing two screws on each hinge with longer screws that penetrate wall studs. If the hinge pins are on the outside of the door, install a set of *hinge enforcers.* These inexpensive devices hold a door in place even when the hinge pins are removed.

Door frames are susceptible to being pried outward, which frees the lock bolt. To defend against this kind of attack, stiffen the door frame by adding plywood shims between the frame and wall studs.

Garage doors are structurally secure, but their locking devices can make them easy targets. When you're away from home, place a padlock in the roller track. If you have an automatic door opener, make sure the remote transmitter uses a rolling code system, which prevents thieves from copying your signal. An electronic keypad can make your garage door as secure and easy to use as your front door. These offer the added safety feature of keyless entry: after you teach your children the code, you won't have to worry about lost or stolen keys.

Glass is both the strength and weakness of windows, in terms of security. An intruder can easily break the glass, but the noise it makes is likely to draw attention. Aside from installing metal bars, there's no way to secure the glass, so make sure your windows can't be opened from the outside. There's a host of inexpensive locks available for every type of window.

You can also secure your windows using simple hardware items, such as screws and dowels. And when it comes to securing sliding glass doors, think of them as a big windows: add extra locks and install screws to prevent the panels from being pried from their tracks.

Everything You Need:

Tools: Hammer, drill, hole saw, spade bit, awl, screwdriver, chisel, utility knife.

Materials: (as needed) Plywood, casing nails, board, hinge, screws, eye bolts, dowel, security devices.

Tips for Securing Doors

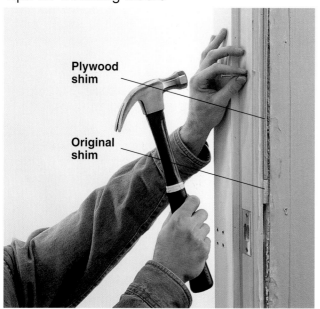

Install plywood shims in the gaps between the door frame and wall studs, to prevent pry-bar attacks. Remove the casing molding on the inside of the frame and inspect the gap; if it's wider than ¼", install new plywood shims in the spaces between the original shims. Be sure to shim directly above, below, and behind the strike plate. Drill pilot holes, and secure the shims with 10d casing nails.

Replace short hinge screws with longer screws (3" or 4") that extend through the door jamb and into the wall studs. This helps resist door kick-ins. Tighten the screws snug, but avoid overtightening them, which can pull the frame out of square.

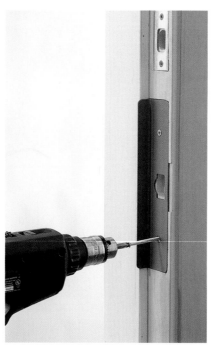

Add metal door reinforcers to strengthen the areas around locks and prevent kick-ins. Remove the lockset (page 150) and slip the reinforcer over the door's edge. Be sure to get a reinforcer that is the correct thickness for your door.

Add a heavy-duty latch guard to reinforce the door jamb around the strike plate. For added protection, choose a guard with a flange that resists pry-bar attacks. Install the guard with long screws that reach the wall studs.

Have lock cylinders re-keyed to ensure that lost or stolen keys can't be used by unwanted visitors. Remove the cylinder (see step 4, page 150), leaving the bolt mechanism in the door, and take it to a locksmith.

How to Install a Deadbolt Lock

1 Measure up from the floor or existing lockset to locate the lock: its center should be at least 3½" from the lockset center. Tape the template (supplied with lock) to the door. Use an awl to mark the centerpoints of the cylinder and deadbolt holes on the door. Close the door and use the template to mark the centerline for the deadbolt hole in the door jamb.

2 Bore the cylinder hole with a hole saw and drill. To avoid splintering the door, drill through one side until the hole saw pilot (mandrel) just comes out the other side. Remove the hole saw, then complete the hole from the opposite side of the door.

3 Use a spade bit to bore the deadbolt hole from the edge of the door into the cylinder hole. Be sure to keep the drill perpendicular to the door edge while drilling.

4 Insert the deadbolt into the edge hole. Fit the two halves of the lock to the door, aligning the cylinder tailpiece and connecting screw fittings with the proper holes in the deadbolt. Secure the two halves together with the connecting screws.

5 Use the centerline mark on the jamb to locate the hole for the deadbolt. Bore the hole, then chisel a mortise for the strike plate (see steps 1 & 2, page 151). Install the strike plate. Or, for greater security, install a security box strike (page 151), instead of the standard strike plate.

How to Install a Security Box Strike

1 Mark the horizontal center of the deadbolt on the doorjamb and tape the box strike template to the jamb, aligning the center marks. Use an awl to mark the drilling points, then use a utility knife to score a ⅛"-deep line around the outside of the template.

2 Drill pilot holes for the faceplate screws, and bore holes for the box mortise, using the recommended spade bit. To chisel the faceplate mortise, make parallel cuts ⅛" deep, holding the chisel at a 45° angle with the bevel side in. Flip the chisel over, and drive it downward to remove the material.

3 Insert the box strike into the mortise and install the screws inside the box. Angle the screws slightly toward the center of the wall stud, to increase their holding power. Position the faceplate and install the screws.

Tips for Securing Sliding Glass Doors

Make a custom lock for your door track, using a thick board and a hinge. Cut the board to fit behind the closed door, then cut it again a few inches from one end. Install a hinge so you can flip up the end and keep the door secure while it's ajar. Attach knobs for easy lifting.

Drive screws into the upper track to keep the sliding panel from being pried up and out of the lower track. Use sturdy panhead screws, spaced about every 8", and drive them so their heads just clear the top of the door. For metal door frames, use self-tapping screws and a low drill speed.

Install a deadbolt lock to the frame of the sliding panel. Drill a hole for the deadbolt into the upper track. Then, drill an additional hole a few inches away so you can lock the door in an open position.

How to Install a Keypad Entry System for a Garage Door

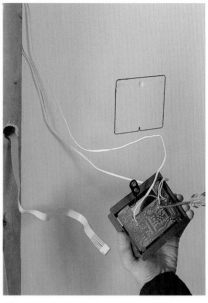

1 Drill an access hole for the keypad cable through the side jamb of the garage door. Make sure there is enough clearance around the hole for mounting the keypad unit. For one-piece doors, you may need to mount the keypad on the front edge of the jamb or on the front garage wall.

2 Feed the keypad cable through the access hole. Position the keypad against the jamb and make marks for the mounting screws. Drill pilot holes for the screws, and mount the keypad.

3 Attach one low-voltage wire to the screw terminals marked 1 and 2 on the back of the new opener console. This wire will connect to the opener unit. Attach another wire to the console terminals marked 1 and 3, then attach the other end of that wire to the screw terminals on the plug-in transformer.

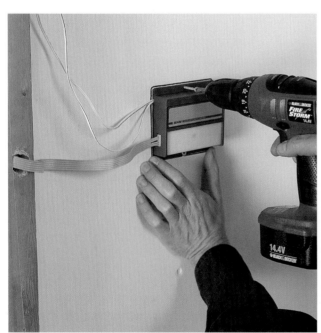

4 Install the battery (for back-up power) in the console and plug the keypad cable into the console outlet. Mount the console to the interior garage wall, about 12" from the door opening. Run the low-voltage wire from the console to the opener unit. Fasten the wire to the wall and ceiling with insulated wire staples.

5 Unplug the opener unit or shut off power at the main service panel (page 33), then remove the access cover on the unit housing. Connect the wire ends to the screw terminals used for the push button controls. Reattach the access cover and restore power to the unit. Plug the transformer into a 120-volt receptacle. Program the entry code according to the manufacturer's directions.

Tips for Securing Windows

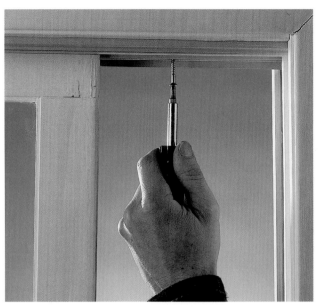

Pin together sashes of single- and double-hung windows with ¼" × 3" eye bolts. With the window closed, drill a ¼"-dia. hole, at a slight downward angle, through the top rail of the bottom sash and into the bottom rail of the top sash. Avoid hitting the glass, and stop the hole about ¾ of the way through the top sash. To lock the window in open positions, drill holes along the sash stiles (vertical pieces) instead.

Drive screws into the top channel of sliding windows to prevent intruders from lifting the window sash out of the lower channel. The screws should just clear the top of the window and not interfere with its operation. Use sturdy screws, and space them about 6" apart.

Block sash channels on sliding windows with a narrow board or a thick dowel.

Use auxiliary locks on sliding windows when a dowel or board won't work. Most types can be installed on the upper or lower window track.

Replace old sash locks on double hung windows with keyed devices. Traditional sash locks can be highly vulnerable–especially on old windows. Be sure to store a key nearby, for emergency exits.

Installing Security Lighting

As a practical crime deterrent, nothing is more effective than a light. And outdoor lighting is as useful for making a house safe to come home to as it is for repelling burglars. To determine where lighting is needed, give your house a thorough after-dark inspection, noting any areas where someone might lurk out of view from the street or from inside the house.

A good lighting plan should include a light at each entrance, with some lighting on all four sides of the house, as well as around the garage. But that doesn't mean you have to light up your yard like a ball park. In fact, lights that are too bright can create dark shadows outside of the light's beam. The objective, then, is to illuminate the grounds with relatively low, ambient light, and use brighter, more focused lighting for entrances and motion detection.

As with interior lighting, energy-efficient outdoor lights are always a good option. Motion-detector lights not only cut down on energy costs, they're doubly effective as security lights: the sudden blast of light surprises intruders and catches your attention.

Everything You Need:

Tools: Screwdrivers, neon circuit tester.

Materials: Motion detector light fixture.

Tips for Improving Security Lighting

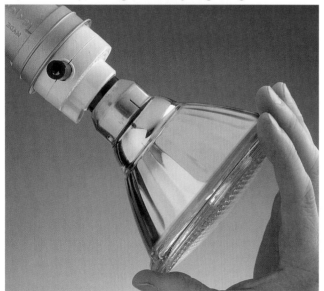

Photo sensitive lights automatically turn on at dusk and off at dawn, making them ideal for energy-efficient exterior lighting when you're away from home. Many devices are simply sockets that screw into standard light fixtures.

Timer switches let you control interior lights automatically, so you never have to come home to a dark house. Some types have random switching that simulates normal lighting habits when no one is home.

How to Replace an Exterior Light with a Motion-Detector Light

Whenever possible, install motion-detector lights out-of-reach from the ground. Security lights are most effective if they can't be tampered with. Also, a light brightens a larger area from a higher position.

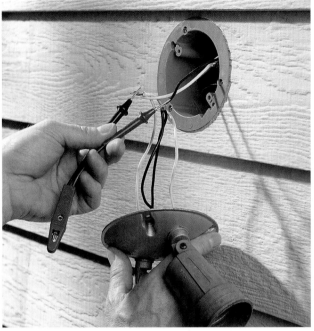

1 Shut off the power to the fixture at the main service panel (page 33). Remove the screws securing the fixture to its electrical box. Without touching any bare wire ends, remove the wire connectors joining the black and white circuit wires to the fixture leads, and test for power with a neon circuit tester. Touch one tester probe to the end of each circuit wire. If the tester glows, the power is still on. Return to the service panel and turn off the correct circuit.

2 Disconnect the wires and remove the old fixture. Connect the new fixture, using wire connectors, and following the manufacturer's wiring directions. Be sure the fixture or the electrical box has a weatherproof foam gasket, to seal out water. Secure the fixture's mounting plate to the electrical box.

3 Adjust the range of the motion sensor. Select a setting that is sensitive to motion in a specific area, keeping in mind that frequent trippings of the light will decrease its effectiveness.

Appendix

Converting Measurements

To Convert:	To:	Multiply by:
Inches	Millimeters	25.4
Inches	Centimeters	2.54
Feet	Meters	0.305
Yards	Meters	0.914
Square inches	Square centimeters	6.45
Square feet	Square meters	0.093
Square yards	Square meters	0.836
Cubic inches	Cubic centimeters	16.4
Cubic feet	Cubic meters	0.0283
Cubic yards	Cubic meters	0.765
Ounces	Milliliters	30.0
Pints (U.S.)	Liters	0.473 (Imp. 0.568)
Quarts (U.S.)	Liters	0.946 (Imp. 1.136)
Gallons (U.S.)	Liters	3.785 (Imp. 4.546)
Ounces	Grams	28.4
Pounds	Kilograms	0.454

To Convert:	To:	Multiply by:
Millimeters	Inches	0.039
Centimeters	Inches	0.394
Meters	Feet	3.28
Meters	Yards	1.09
Square centimeters	Square inches	0.155
Square meters	Square feet	10.8
Square meters	Square yards	1.2
Cubic centimeters	Cubic inches	0.061
Cubic meters	Cubic feet	35.3
Cubic meters	Cubic yards	1.31
Milliliters	Ounces	.033
Liters	Pints (U.S.)	2.114 (Imp. 1.76)
Liters	Quarts (U.S.)	1.057 (Imp. 0.88)
Liters	Gallons (U.S.)	0.264 (Imp. 0.22)
Grams	Ounces	0.035
Kilograms	Pounds	2.2

Drill Bit Guide

Twist Bit   **Carbide-tipped Masonry**   **Glass & Tile**   **Spade Bit**   **Adjustable Counterbore**   **Hole Saw**

Counterbore, Shank & Pilot Hole Diameters

Screw Size	Counterbore Diameter for Screw Head	Clearance Hole for Screw Shank	Pilot Hole Diameter	
			Hard Wood	Soft Wood
#1	9/64	5/64	3/64	1/32
#2	1/4	3/32	3/64	1/32
#3	1/4	7/64	1/16	3/64
#4	1/4	1/8	1/16	3/64
#5	1/4	1/8	5/64	1/16
#6	5/16	9/64	3/32	5/64
#7	5/16	5/32	3/32	5/64
#8	3/8	11/64	1/8	3/32
#9	3/8	11/64	1/8	3/32
#10	3/8	3/16	1/8	7/64
#11	1/2	3/16	5/32	9/64
#12	1/2	7/32	9/64	1/8

Additional Resources

Behr Process Corp.
Santa Ana, CA 92704
800-854-0133

Chimney Safety Institute of America
8752 Robbins Rd.
Indianapolis, IN 46268
800-536-0118
www.csia.org

Gypsum Association
810 First St., NE, #510
Washington DC 20002
202-289-5440
www.gypsum.org

Kwikset Corporation
516 East Santa Ana St.
Anaheim, CA 92803
714-535-8111
www.blackanddecker.com

Minwax
10 Mountainview Rd.
Upper Saddle River, NJ 07458
www.minwax.com

National Lighting Bureau
Communications Office
8811 Colesville Rd.
Suite G106
Silver Spring, MD 20910
301-587-9572
www.nlb.org

National Wood Flooring Association
800-422-4556
www.woodfloors.org

Quikrete
2987 Clairmont Rd.
Suite 500
Atlanta, GA 30329
404-634-9100
www.quikrete.com

Tile Council of America
P.O. Box 1787
Clemson, SC 29633
864-646-8453
www.tileusa.com

U.S. Environmental Protection Agency
Indoor Air Quality
www.epa.gov/iedweb00/pubs/insidest.html

Additional Reading From Creative Publishing international:

The Complete Photo Guide to Home Repair
The Complete Guide to Home Plumbing
The Complete Guide to Home Wiring
Exterior Home Repairs & Improvements
Home Masonry Repairs & Projects
Popular Mechanics: Houseworks
Today's Homeowner: Essential Home Tips

INDEX

Creative Publishing international, Inc.
offers a variety of how-to books. For
information, write or visit our website:

Creative Publishing international, Inc.
Subscriber Books
5900 Green Oak Drive
Minnetonka, MN 55343

www.creativepub.com